Silence: A User's Guide

Also by Maggie Ross

Silence: A User's Guide, Volume 1: Process

Writing the Icon of the Heart

Seasons of Death and Life

Pillars of Flame

The Fountain and the Furnace

The Fire of Your Life

Silence: A User's Guide

Volume 2: Application

MAGGIE ROSS

CASCADE *Books* · Eugene, Oregon

SILENCE: A USER'S GUIDE
Volume 2: Application

Cascade Books
An Imprint of Wipf and Stock Publishers
199 W. 8th Ave., Suite 3
Eugene, OR 97401

www.wipfandstock.com

PAPERBACK ISBN: 978-1-62564-797-9
HARDCOVER ISBN: 978-1-4982-8795-1
EBOOK ISBN: 978-1-5326-1208-4

Cataloguing-in-Publication data:

Names: Ross, Maggie

Title: Silence: a user's guide : volume 2: application / Maggie Ross.

Description: Eugene, OR: Cascade Books, 2018 | Includes bibliographical references.

Identifiers: ISBN 978-1-62564-797-9 (paperback) | ISBN 978-1-4982-8795-1 (hardcover)
| ISBN 978-1-5326-1208-4 (ebook)

Subjects: LCSH: Silence—Religious aspects—Christianity | Spiritual life—Christianity |
Spirituality

Classification: BV4509.5 R67 2018 (print) | BV4509.5 (ebook)

Manufactured in the U.S.A.   11/06/17

The author gratefully acknowledges The Beinecke Rare Book and Manuscript
Library, Yale University, for the cover illustration from the Rothchild Canticles.

All biblical quotations are from the Revised Standard Common Bible translation,
unless otherwise noted.

Boydell and Brewer has given permission to reuse and dissect the paper "The
Apophatic Image: The Poetics of Effacement in Julian of Norwich," first published
in Marion Glasscoe (ed.), The Medieval Mystical Tradition in England V. Wood-
bridge, UK: Boydell & Brewer, 1992.

This book is dedicated to
Vincent Gillespie
J. R. R. Tolkien Professor of English Language and Literature
in the University of Oxford
and to
Pauline Matarasso
Scholar, Mentor, Friend

Behold, Lord, the waves of thy grace
close my mouth with silence, and there is not a thought left in me,
not even for giving thanks unto thee.

Contents

Introduction

IN THIS VOLUME WE turn to texts, liturgy, and beholding. It has been a very difficult book to write, as having discussed silence at length in Volume 1, it is as if I myself have been silenced. But there is merit in looking into texts and liturgy to apply the model of the mind described in the first volume on the work of silence, the self-forgetfulness that leads to beholding, and the transfiguration that is its consequence.

Books are often full of surprises for their authors and this one was no exception. Perhaps the biggest surprise was that chapter 3 turned itself into an exposition of New Testament texts on glory, that *kenosis* is *glory.* That *kenosis* is glory has been a theme in my writing since the beginning, but this is the most explicit demonstration yet. The thread of the glory of the human person as the other side of the *kenosis* coin runs through the New Testament and much of the Old, but it has been badly neglected and needs to be foregrounded, especially in our age when the degradation of the human person is ubiquitous, and the grinding pressure of consumerism relentless. Given the political erosion of democracy that is taking place in many countries, understanding the glory and transfiguration of the human person becomes ever more important and subversive.

To learn to read a text for the portals of silence that are implicit is to gain a powerful tool for supporting and expanding one's silence, and to open the reader to the insight that ensues. I hesitate to use the phrase *lectio divina* because of the pious musings often associated with it. The sort of reading I am proposing in this volume is a far cry from such manipulations, and is both more costly and more rewarding. Once again, these pages invite readers to look at their own minds, to reflect on what is happening there, and to understand the essential role of silence for being human, and for living our own truth with one another.

Chapter One discusses reading texts in general and reading for silence in particular, and suggests a rather unorthodox reading of the Pseudo-Dionysius.

Chapter Two suggests ways of reading the Old Testament for its silences so that the subversive Old Testament God may be revealed.

Chapter Three looks at the New Testament, which is explicit in its discussion of the model of the mind presented in Volume 1, and the glory to which it is the key.

Chapter Four discusses ways that silence could and should be restored to liturgy and why. It gives an example of a catechetical rite that takes the participants to the roots of Eucharist from which other forms of liturgy may emerge.

Chapter Five is an *ecomium* on the word *behold* and contains a short conclusion.

The rest is silence.

Feast of the Transfiguration, 2017

ONE

Textual Silence

Silence is a mystery of the age to come,
but words are instruments of this world. . . .
[K]now that every loquacious man is inwardly empty,
though he discourse on amazing things . . .
If you love the truth, love silence.
This will make you illumined in God . . .
and will deliver you from the illusions of ignorance.
Silence unites you to God himself.

—ISAAC OF NINEVEH[1]

The ancient and medieval view of scriptural and ritual symbols
involved both subtle theories of the cognitive process and the convic-
tion that this process was not just a matter of human will and skill
but a spiritual journey through the symbols to God.

—PAUL ROREM[2]

. . . the Aristotelian sect is now dominant, which thinks the coin-
cidence of opposites heresy, while the admission of such a heresy is
the beginning of mystic theology. Theirs is a science which lies in
disputatious exercises and it seeks a victory of words (by which) it is
inflated: "inflatus vanitate verbalis scientiae."

—NICHOLAS OF CUSA[3]

[handwritten marginalia: "a Thing cannot be & not be at The Same Time"]

---

1. Isaac of Nineveh, *Ascetical Homilies*, Homilies 65 and 64 (pp. 221 and 207). The translation is in prose but I have set it as poetry for emphasis. Note that "the age to come" refers not to pie in the sky by and by, but rather to the kingdom of heaven that is within and available to each person who is willing to do the work of silence.

2. Rorem, *Biblical and Liturgical Symbols*, 10.

3. Cranz, *Nicholas of Cusa*, 26.

1

In Volume 1 of this book, we looked at the model of two aspects of knowing, which optimally work together, ideally becoming a single, seamless, reciprocal flow between self-conscious mind and deep mind, each informing and enhancing the other—what I have called *the work of silence*. It is not necessary to believe anything to embark on the work of silence, even if it is being used only for the purpose of engaging a text (or work of art); but it should be noted that the act of letting go one's preconceptions is the same for nonbeliever and believer alike. This process entails relinquishing the modern solipsistic notion of "experience" that sets up preconceptions and expectations, which are inimical to inhabiting a text or the transfiguration (change of perspective, the way we "figure things out") of perspective.

Sebastian Brock describes Ephrem's fourth-century journey through the various modes of knowing. His receptivity and openness is a model for working with the tropes and silences of ancient, patristic, and medieval texts: that is, engagement and reciprocity between the two aspects of knowing. For the nonbeliever, Ephrem's "God," "commerce," "meditation," and "reciprocity" can refer simply to deep mind or truth. His "love and wonder," however, have no substitute, for they have been acknowledged as the foundation of philosophy from the time of the ancient Greeks to this day. We must also remember that until approximately the twelfth century what we today call theology was then called philosophy, and it was understood that there was no philosophy/theology without praxis, without working with the mind by means of what I am calling "the work of silence":

> Theology, like any other intellectual pursuit, can take on three different forms, depending on the attitude of mind present in the person setting out on the path of enquiry. In the first place the mind may seek to *dominate and subjugate* the object of its enquiry. Such an attitude has characterized much scientific and other enquiry from the time of Francis Bacon onwards. Whether rightly or wrongly, Ephrem saw this as the basic attitude of many "heretical" thinkers of his own time: in the field of theology, in particular, such intellectual pride is utterly abhorrent to him.
>
> A second approach takes on what at first seems a much more acceptable form, a form that is typical of much theological enquiry today: here the mind sets out to study the object of its enquiry in as *dispassionate and "scientific" a way as possible.* It is an approach that in many spheres is of course very fruitful, and

it is one that Ephrem implies that he himself tried—but found wanting: "Turn me back to Your teaching: I wanted to stand back, but I saw that I became the poorer. For the soul does not get any benefit except through converse with You" (*Faith* 32:1).

The third approach, which is Ephrem's, is that of *engagement above all of love and wonder.* Whereas the second approach involves only a one-way movement, from the mind to the object of enquiry, this third approach is a two-way affair, *involving a continual interaction.* Only by means of such an interaction of love can human knowledge of divine truth grow. Ephrem continues in the same hymn:

> Whenever I have meditated upon You
> I have acquired a veritable treasure from You;
> Whatever aspect of You I have contemplated,
> a stream has flowed from You.
> There is no way in which I can contain it:
>
> Your fountain, Lord, is hidden
> from the person who does not thirst for You;
> Your treasury seems empty
> to the person who rejects You.
> Love is the treasurer
> of your heavenly treasure store (*Faith* 32:2–3).

The way in which we perceive both God and the created world about us thus depends on our basic attitude and approach, whether as objects of enquiry somehow separate from our selves, or whether we see our selves as irrevocably involved in the object of our enquiry—and, in the case of theology, whether we are willing to participate in the mystery concerned. Ephrem is in no doubt that where knowledge of God is sought, this last way is not only the only acceptable way, but also the only possible one.[4]

In volume one of the present work, we saw how this optimal relationship is a perennial threat to institutions and those who support them, for the work of silence makes people incoercible. We saw, too, how the medieval church came to suppress the knowledge of the work of silence with catastrophic consequences for Western Christianity, and the humanities and sciences down to and including the present day. We saw how, in consequence, some interpreters mistake method for philosophy when reading pre-fifteenth-century texts and some modern texts (e.g.,

---

4. Brock, *Luminous Eye*, 43–44, italics mine.

Simone Weil), and that without this knowledge translators make egregious errors in their rendering of these texts.

In addition, we noted how translations have become flattened, and how this flattening has affected negatively the creation of many modern analytical texts as well as literature. We have also looked at the problem of the anachronistic insertion of the word "experience" into many of these translations, and how emphasis on modern notions of experience are contrary to both the intent and meaning of these texts. We looked at the roots of these problems, which are found in the distancing of human beings from the natural world into which they were once integrated, so that they understand neither their own world nor that of the other, whether that other is the ecology, another person, a text, or approaches to the divine.

In Volume 2, I would like to turn to various applications of the model of the work of silence. I will give examples of how ancient and medieval authors used various tropes to finesse and subvert the self-reflexive linearity of language, and how the modern reader can use the work of silence to enter more deeply into texts, both as reader and writer. In part, this involves reading texts as poetry, such as Bernard of Clairvaux's sermons on the Song of Songs, for example, even if they are set out as prose; for their uses of metaphor, hyperbole, and self-subversion, along with other tropes, are misconstrued if they are taken at face value or read "literally." They rather have to be read literarily.

In 1992, Vincent Gillespie and I published a paper entitled "The Apophatic Image: The Poetics of Effacement in Julian of Norwich." This paper was well received, as were Gillespie's "Postcards from the Edge" (1992) and my "Apophatic Prayer as a Theological Model" (1993) However, it has become clear over the past two decades that many readers have not entirely understood the foundational principles outlined in these papers, which relate to the work of silence. In consequence, in 2011, Vincent Gillespie asked me to write the paper that became "Behold Not the Cloud of Experience" (2013), a prequel to the other three papers. The themes from this last paper have already been partly explored in Volume 1, but I would like to begin Volume 2 by reverting to some of the main points of the original paper, "The Apophatic Image," from which the other papers have sprung.

It may seem paradoxical to analyze a paper that attempts to encourage readers to allow their analytic faculty to be destabilized, bypassed, and negated; to understand that paradoxes must be allowed to stand because they bring the linear and discursive mind to a halt so that deep mind has an opportunity to bring its holistic perspective to bear; or to suggest general categories for some of the tropes that seek precisely to transgress categorical boundaries. But the Cartesian methodology in which most students are trained binds them with a chain whose links are very difficult to break, and thus a certain amount of explanation in their own terms seems necessary to pry them open. In addition, Vincent Gillespie's and my understanding of the impact and nuances of certain words has both expanded and clarified, and it might be useful to show how certain terms have carried over—or have been discarded or changed—since 1992–93. As I cannot speak for Gillespie, these changes reflect my views alone, although he has seen what I have written and is happy with it.

For example, what we called "apophatic consciousness" in 1992, I now call "deep mind"; the terms are interchangeable:

> To enter apophatic consciousness, the seeker must simultane-
> ously desire it intensely and give up all desire. This paradox
> is deliberately subversive. It threatens the logical, hierarchical
> command and control structures that motivate the human
> need to resolve, categorise and classify. It challenges our sense
> of the ordinary, threatens our usual interpretative patterns and
> displaces our dominant modes of perception. Like the self-
> emptying humility of Christ on the Cross it defies reconciliation
> to the logic of the world. It is a sign of contradiction, allowing
> the creative tension between its conflicting significations to
> generate a precious stillness, a chink in the defensive wall of
> reason that allows slippage into apophatic consciousness.[5] [This
> approach echoes T. S. Eliot's line about caring/not caring and
> sitting still. To read in this way is not a short-cut; it is rather a
> quantum leap.][6]

Although in some ways "apophatic consciousness" is a better phrase, I switched to "deep mind" for several reasons: first, the word *apophatic* is unfamiliar to some readers, while for other readers, it has been overused to the point that it is almost as useless as the term *mystical* and its cognates. It also seems to have taken on the nuance of leaving ordinary life in a sort of "minds cut off from bodies" aspect.

Apophatic can refer to a method of argument, to the effacement of images, to the relinquishing of images, to iconoclasm, and to understanding

5. Gillespie and Ross, "The Apophatic Image," 56.
6. Gillespie and Ross, "'With mekeness aske perseverantly,'" 126–41.

and insight given in consequences of the self-emptying of *kenosis*—these are but a few of its uses. In addition, there are myriad problems with the word *consciousness*: modern authors often limit it to reflexivity, to self-consciousness, without distinguishing the various modes of consciousness or awareness it entails. In no way is "apophatic consciousness" an "altered state" or trance or other deviation from ordinary life. It optimally works seamlessly and reciprocally with self-conscious mind. This holistic process results in living the ordinary through transfigured perception.

"Apophatic consciousness" also can be confusing in that, as we have seen in the previous volume, the self-conscious mind identifies and categorizes what it encounters by an apophatic process, by telling itself what the object is *not*. In addition, the deep mind, which perceives directly, is itself apophatic, hidden from what we perceive as our selves, that is to say, our ideas of our selves which the self-conscious mind constructs: our self-consciousness cannot directly access or control deep mind, although to a certain extent our self-consciousness can influence through intention some of what deep mind thinks about/works on out of our sight: we can learn to work co-operatively with that greater part of the mind that is apophatic to us; that is, hidden from us.

The most difficult aspect of this model for some people, especially scholars, seems to be their inability to accept that *the deep mind/apophatic consciousness is a thinking mind*. It could be argued that the term "deep mind" is somewhat vague, but, as we shall see, deliberate ambiguity is one of the strategies by which writers bypass the linear and reflexive nature of language and speak directly to deep mind. It is a strategy by which self-consciousness subverts itself,[7] and enables language to subvert its own linearity to gesture towards the infinite. Any description or model of the mind can only be linear and is therefore a mere gesture towards that which is *both* linear *and* holographic/holistic.

Furthermore, for reasons already discussed in Volume 1, not only should the term *mystical* be dropped from usage, we also should be extremely careful about using the word *experience* in the modern sense.

---

7. In the previous volume, we saw that the self-conscious mind employs one-pointed meditation (for example) to subvert itself: exploiting its ability to focus tightly, it concentrates on one word to enable itself to relinquish its own thoughts, strategies, etc., and to open to receive from deep mind. To put this another way, it uses a word to get rid of words so that it can listen to the Word. It should be noted, however, that this relinquishment is only a *seeming*, for opening to deep mind allows the contents of self-conscious mind to be refined and integrated by deep mind, and to transfigure the perceptions of self-conscious mind.

Experience is *always* interpretation, and refers exclusively to the processes of self-reflection, interpretation, and categorization. For these reasons, the terms "contemplative experience" (or text, or discourse), and "mystical" experience (or text or discourse) are nonsensical, for contemplation strictly speaking requires the relinquishing of all claims to experience. Even the awareness that there has been an "experience" is already interpretation. If there has been an occurrence of *excessus mentis* (complete self-forgetfulness), merely noticing that something "has happened" by way of the traces that may be left after the fact—for example, the passage of time unawares—is already interpretation.

When the model of the two aspects of knowing—the work of silence—has not been used in reading a text, the word *experience* is often wrongly inserted into translations, as in Grover Zinn's translation of Richard of St Victor, and James Walsh's translation of *The Cloud of Unknowing* (both volumes in the Classics of Western Spirituality series).[8] What is more, many people seem to use *experience* almost without thinking, for want of the effort to find another word. In spite of claims to the contrary (*pace* E. A. Jones), there are plenty of words that can be used to avoid a misuse of *experience*, such as "incident" or "incidence," "occasion," "moment," "engagement," "occurrence": e.g., "There was an incident (or occurrence, or moment) of *excessus mentis* (complete self-forgetfulness)"; or "he described the traces left by an occasion of self-forgetfulness"; or "the momentary loss of self-consciousness left traces in her memory"; or "she returned to herself." *Excessus mentis* is not an extraordinary occurrence; it happens many times a day in the ordinary course of things and is essential to the learning process.

Similar principles also apply when grouping certain kinds of texts: for example, the term "English mystics" is extremely misleading when used to gather together texts as early as the *Ancrene Wisse* (c. 1224–35) and as late as Julian of Norwich and Nicholas Love (d. 1424), for among these texts only those authored by *The Cloud of Unknowing* writer, along with Julian's *Showings* (Long Text) are truly anagogical: they actually invite readers into the "space" of contemplation and encourage them to remain there *without filling up that space with pious thoughts, manufactured emotion, devotional words, set prayers, or kitsch "spirituality."*

The other texts commonly placed in this group are trance-inducing (e.g., Richard Rolle), didactic (Walter Hilton), and visionary/devotional

---

8. In addition to the discussion in Volume 1, see "Behold Not the Cloud of Experience."

(Margery Kempe). If we look at Continental writers, we can add the category of those that are abstract (*Imitation of Christ*). These are but a few ways such texts might be more accurately categorized than they have been in the past.[9]

In the first volume, we also noted the need for a greater precision with words: for example, the distinction among the words *transfigure, transcend,* and *transform* is critical. In the crudest terms, *transfigure* refers to a gratuitous insight arising from deep mind, resulting in a shift in perspective: nothing is left behind or denied. The latter two words are dualistic; they even carry nuances of magic.[10] These words are, in any event, anti-incarnational. Rather, grace leaves nothing behind. Humans are not changed from one thing into something else: frogs are not made into prince or princesses. Indeed, the parts of our selves we dislike the most are precisely our means of sanctification. Even to say God "transcends" the creation in which he is immanent is dualistic: it dismantles the necessary paradox of transcendence/immanence of a God simultaneously beyond being and intimate within being in all its forms.

We have also seen that a merely linear approach to ancient, patristic, and medieval texts that are based on a two-aspects-of-knowing model of the mind can lead to a scholar's completely missing the mark, as with Karsten Harries' analyses of Meister Eckhart and Nicholas of Cusa. Harries' primary error is to mistake these two authors' discussions of method for philosophy. Similar errors have been committed by those who have worked on the ancestor of these two writers, the Pseudo-Dionysius, who will be discussed later in this chapter.

It is essential to be exact about the terms we use when writing about these and other ancient and medieval texts, for as every student was once taught (but no longer is), attention to the way a text is constructed and the psychological resonances not only of individual words but of syntax are just as important, if not more important, in communicating content than observing the rules of grammar. The modern author, Marilynne Robinson (*Gilead, Home, Lila*) is but one of the contemporary advocates

---

9. We might add "medicinal," a category that overarches these distinctions: see the work of Daniel McCann, *Soul Health: Therapeutic Reading in Late Medieval England* (forthcoming).

10. Magic as it is commonly understood is antithetical to Christianity: Christianity releases a person to open to many futures, while magic attempts to confine a person to a single deterministic future.

for return to this lost art, this careful attention, which must be restored to writing in general and academic writing in particular.

———◆———

The first sign in "The Apophatic Image" is that of the empty mercy seat, "the great speaking absence between the cherubim."[11] In that paper we confine our discussion to the paradox of the flickering divine presence/absence that the image evokes, and to "become the word uttered by God, the prayer prayed by God through us."[12] This image of the space between the cherubim is one of the richest and most resonant in biblically based writing. Perhaps its most eloquent Christian exponent is Richard of St Victor, thought to be a Scot by origin, who died in 1173. Richard wrote a treatise on contemplation that is commonly known as *The Mystical Ark*.[13] He was greatly influenced by the Pseudo-Dionysius (who worked in the late fifth and early sixth centuries), and in turn influenced such figures as Bonaventure (1221–74) and Dante (1265–1321). The treatise is an excellent example of theology and psychological method coinhered.

The text reveals that Richard had an acute understanding of what I have called "the work of silence." His exploration arises not from modern solipsistic ideas of "experience," but rather from a detached observation and testing of his own mind, combined with his extensive reading of the biblical tradition, the patristic tradition available to him, and the works his predecessor Hugh of St Victor—all of which describe, under various guises, the work of silence.

The mercy seat echoes and conflates all the life-giving empty places in the Bible: the empty tomb, Elijah's cave, the womb of Mary, to name but three. It expresses the ancient meaning of "salvation," which is to be freed from a trap and brought into an open space. It is the place where God speaks to the heart (Exod 25:22). It gestures towards the liminal in

11. Williams, *Open to Judgement*, 112–17, 85.

12. Gillespie and Ross, "The Apophatic Image," 55.

13. The treatise has been translated by Grover Zinn in the joint edition published by Paulist Press and SPCK in 1979: *Richard of St Victor: The Twelve Patriarchs, The Mystical Ark, Book Three of the Trinity*. It should be noted, however, that while Zinn understands beholding, his translation is consistently misleading because he uses the word *experience* in such nonsensical phrases as "an experience of *excessus mentis*," as discussed above and in Volume 1. Steven Chase, in his study of *The Mystical Ark*, also misuses this word in a similar way, and his otherwise interesting study is flawed by presuming to insert his own solipsistic *experience* (in the modern sense) into his analysis. See Chase, *Angelic Wisdom*.

each person, who, walking through the gates of paradox,[14] is opened to receive what deep mind has to offer; the deep mind where dwells our shared nature with God. We enter deep mind through the open gate of liminal space, the consequence of *kenosis*, detachment, an emptying of all of one's ideas, concepts, and "knowledge" (in the linear, self-conscious, everyday sense) to focus attention wholly on what is given beyond self-consciousness. "This is the Passover . . . [by which] the soul must cast off the restrictions of language and cross the Jordan from discursive consciousness [self-consciousness] to apophatic consciousness [deep mind] in which will be found the promised land of truth."[15]

The cherubim are polysemous in meaning. Among their primary significations is unity in diversity. Steven Chase refers to this unity as "dialectical integration." Among the strategies and paradoxes that find their unity in this figure are all of the methods of biblical interpretation; for the medieval reader this included the "literal, allegorical, anagogical and tropological senses of scripture, which are mutually [inter]dependent and related. . . . This reintegration is constant prayer."[16] As these schemes and systems of categorization are broken down, care must be taken by the reader that he or she does not substitute new ones in their place. For example, in Julian of Norwich's *Long Text*:

> To replace the traditional fourfold categories of scriptural exegesis with new categories reflecting apparently major strands in [Julian's] text (for example: narrative, biblical, theological, and apophatic) would be to reduce into strata a text that deliberately aspires towards the complexity of the molecular.[17]

Essential to understanding this approach is that texts such as this

> invite us to enter a relational universe. . . . [Such texts] refuse "to accept any reality that could be frozen motionless. . . . [They seek] to enact a nonlinear dynamic that is the world suffused, enfolded and sustained, . . . nonlinearity means that the act of playing the game has a way of changing the rules."[18]

14. Paradox is paradoxical only to the linear, self-conscious mind. Deep mind is inclusive, what ancient writers refer to as the place of unity. Its ways of thinking are holistic, even holographic. See the discussion in chapter 2 of Volume 1.

15. Gillespie and Ross, "The Apophatic Image," 55.

16. Chase, Angelic Wisdom, 59.

17. Gillespie and Ross, "The Apophatic Image," 58. The word "molecular" refers to a multi-dimensional dynamic.

18. Ibid., 57. Quotation from Gleick, *Chaos*.

This is not a new approach, as can be seen from Sebastian Brock's discussion of paradox in Ephrem's fourth-century theology with its insistence on nonlinearity:

> How does this theology of paradox work? To illustrate in a simple way the basic difference between what one may call the philosophical approach to theology, with its search for definitions, and the symbolic approach, one may visualize a circle with a point in the centre, where the point represents that aspect of God under enquiry. The philosophical approach seeks to identify and locate this central point, in other words, to define it, set boundaries to it. The symbolic approach, on the other hand, attempts no such thing; rather, it will provide a series of paradoxical pairs of opposites, placing them at opposite points around the circumference of the circle; the central point is left undefined, but something of its nature and whereabouts can be inferred by joining up various opposite points, the different paradoxes, on the circle's circumference. The former procedure can be seen as providing a static understanding of the centre point, while the latter offers an understanding that remains essentially dynamic in character.[19]

Richard's *Mystical Ark* emphasizes this dynamic, both the motion and the global polyvalence. Chase summarizes "*coincidentia oppositorum* and contemplative hovering."

> The coincidence of opposites, or more precisely in Richard's case, the coincidence of mutually affirming and denying complementarity, has generally been used to describe the metaphysics of dialectical integration while hovering has generally been used to describe the symbolics of dialectical integration. Both, through the grace of contemplation, draw the contemplative "in" toward divine incomprehensibility, and "out" toward angelization [that is, *theosis*, and the raising up of others, to which human beings are opened by the single focus of their attention. [Chase's clumsy use of the misleading word *angelization* does not mean minds cut off from bodies; rather, quite the reverse: the cherubim are symbolic of holding apparent polarities in unity in one's being], "in" toward wisdom and "out" toward virtue, "in" toward [transfiguration] of consciousness and "out" toward sanctification.[20]

---

19. Brock, *The Luminous Eye*, 24–25.
20. Chase, *Angelic Wisdom*, 131.

Contemplation finds its natural expression outwardly in the self-forgetful service ("virtue") of the other.

> In Richard of St. Victor, flight into contemplative mystery, the symbol of the cherubim, points beyond itself, . . . it is . . . capable of dwelling in paradox. Polysemic, the symbol of the cherubim also manifests the logic or path of participation; the cherubim serve as guides for contemplative journeys of introversion and extroversion, as sacramental images of anagogic daring, and as models of sacred ground . . . they function according to the basic Dionysian typology of similar and dissimilar symbols. As angels, the cherubim are messengers, warriors, protectors and guardians, and symbols of flight, light, praise, and ascent. In Richard's contemplative teaching, the cherubim also symbolize the presence of divine mystery, participation in divine drama, and hovering in divine manifestations of joy and wisdom. In addition, for the contemplative, the cherubim and ark present an icon in the shape and form of a sacred womb that represents the process of the rebirthing . . . .

The word *rebirthing* signifies an anachronistic use of a modern (and dubious) psychological concept that does not exist in the Middle Ages; it is rather what Nicodemus is talking about in John 3:1–21; or what Eckhart calls "the birth of the soul" (in deep mind); or what I have called "the unfolding of the truth of the self" (also in deep mind), of self and the birth of the promise of divine speaking. Explicitly the cherubim symbolize the unity of substance and trinity of persons within the Trinity, and implicitly they symbolize the two natures, God and human, of Christ.[21]

The cherubim and the space between them also hold in unity all the paradoxes of Christianity, of philosophy, of life: divine/human; transcendent/immanent; revealed/concealed; inner/outer; poor/rich; wounded/transfigured; ordinary/extraordinary; gain/loss; dead/alive; secular/holy and all the paradoxes of the Beatitudes (Matt 5:3–12). The mercy seat between the cherubim is a manifestation of what is arguably the most important word in the Bible, *behold*, which has been mentioned in passing throughout the first volume, and which will be discussed at greater length in the last chapter of this book.

"The Apophatic Image" immediately links this first image with another: the empty tomb and the angel's words to Mary Magdalene: "Why seek you the living with the dead?" (Luke 24:5), followed by Christ's

---

21. Chase, *Angelic Wisdom*, 130.

injunction, *Noli me tangere* (John 20:17). These vignettes signal a seismic shift, not only in perspective, but also in the way that "seeking to the beholding" is undertaken. The Father has not only released Christ from the bondage of the tomb, but Christ has released human beings from the binding (*religatio*) of the law, from the oppression of materialized religion and fallen language. The en-Christing process,[22] the Way, the work of silence, leads the person willing to commit to the unknowing of faith out of bondage. This commitment to unknowing frees a person from the unstable play of presence and absence in religion and language, and moves them into unbounded spaciousness and a very different sort of play with the divine (*eutrapelia*, "gamesumli play" in the *Cloud of Unknowing*) of resurrection in this life.[23]

> The play of absence and presence characterizes the human experience of engagement with the ineffable. The search for the Transcendental Signified which is God requires not only a struggle with the fallen will but also the necessity of wrestling with a fallen language which resolutely anchors itself in the world of signifiers. . . . The game of . . . hide and seek acted out over the centuries generates a longing for release from the play of language.[24]

There is a fundamental paradox here: the more human beings try to guarantee divine presence through material observances such as the law, devotion, or the modern consumer cult of generating artificial and self-oriented "experiences," the more they are confronted with a sense of absence. To be freed from the flicker of presence and absence requires a move into the unbounded spaciousness of the deep mind, opened to us through the liminal. Having left language and self-consciousness behind, we realize the integration of our shared nature with God. This is not impossible because

> . . . Christ's lapse into language in the incarnation is his own freely given sacrifice of his ineffable nature on the altar of human meaning. The incarnation of the *logos* allows him to speak to us and through us and to redeem our language through his words. The Word becomes the bridge between voice and silence, the means of passing over from the earthly signification

---

22. Jesus was a person; Christ is the en-Christing process—see Volume 1, chapter 2.
23. See Rahner, *Man at Play*.
24. Gillespie and Ross, "The Apophatic Image," 53.

of unmediated truth. . . . God's silence spoke with our voice so
that we might hear.[25]

The interplay between language and silence, the en-Christing process, the work of silence that opens the way for us to hear God's speaking,
requires a *kenosis* of mind and a receptive attentiveness—both active and
passive simultaneously—of mind *and* body. It is active in the perseverance required to hold the focus of attention, and both active and passive
in its receptivity. This process is defined by Philippians 2:5–11:

> Let this mind be among you
> which was in Christ Jesus,
> who, though he was in the form of God,
> did not regard equality with God
> as a thing to be grasped
> but emptied himself
> taking the form of a slave,
> being born in human likeness.
> And being found in human form
> he humbled himself and became obedient
> to the point of death—even death on a cross.
> Therefore God also highly exalted him
> and gave him the name that is above every name.
> So that at the name of Jesus every knee should bend,
> in heaven and on earth and under the earth,
> and every tongue should confess
> that Jesus Christ is Lord,
> to the glory of God the Father. (RSV modified)

In other words, we must give up our habitual agenda by which we
"seek to capture God in language [which is] to seek to enmesh him in
the nets of fallen meaning and understanding."[26] Instead we must realize,
manifest, our participating in our shared nature with God (2 Pet 1:4);
we must with all our heart undertake this same *kenosis*, not literally or
physically, but far more radically by letting go our ideas of our selves,

25. Ibid., 55. "Voice and silence" refers to John the Solitary: "How long shall I be in
the world of the voice and not in the world of the word? For everything that is seen is
voice and is spoken with the voice, but in the invisible world there is no voice, for not
even voice can utter its mystery. How long shall I be voice and not silence, when shall I
depart from the voice, no longer remaining in things which the voice proclaims? When
shall I be raised up to silence, to something which neither voice nor word can bring?"
Translated by Sebastian Brock, "John the Solitary, *On Prayer*," 87.

26. Gillespie and Ross, "The Apophatic Image," 55.

the world around us, and most especially our hard-won notions of who God is or ought to be. This is accomplished not by doing but by focusing our whole being in attentive receptivity to the grace that makes us "other Christs." "No longer do I call you servants, . . . I call you friends, for all that I have heard from my Father I have made known to you" (John 15:15 RSV modified; or John 17:21, "That they may be one as we are one"). This passage from John echoes that of Exodus 25:22 cited above concerning the mercy seat, the empty space between the cherubim, in which God promises to come and speak with Moses, with the difference that the mercy seat between the cherubim now resides within the human heart.

This *kenosis* is the means of our passing over from the earthly signification proper to self-conscious mind to unmediated truth located in the deep mind; and, once we have entered it, to rest in its infinite unfolding. This does not mean the suppression of self-conscious mind but rather its integration. "The Word becomes the bridge between voice and silence, the means of passing over from earthly signification to unmediated truth."[27]

> The paradox of the exalted kenosis of the cross becomes a paradigm for the procedures of the text, for Julian's approach to God and for her relationship to her audience. To inhabit the text, the reader must be prepared to inhabit the paradigm. Both Julian and her readers must put on the mind of Christ. Enclosure in the text will paradoxically deliver the reader into a limitless landscape. But the necessary suspension of preconceptions, hermeneutical models and critical faculties is to undergo a displacement from the "ordinary" and a loss of control that is a form of death.[28]

Thus far I have been writing from a Christian point of view because "The Apophatic Image" concerns a Christian text. But the process the paper describes is a prerequisite not only for Christians but also for anyone who wishes to engage a text at the deepest level, or to understand a painting, or to create. This process is not rocket science: it is utterly simple. But people seem to have difficulty both with simplicity and even more with the relinquishing of control, not to mention perseverance in the single-focused attention required to come to this receptivity. The first principle of reading a text is not to bring a theory to it, to try to control the interpretation, to try to keep at bay the silence essential to reading,

27. Ibid.
28. Ibid., 60.

but rather to abandon theory, to let the text have the initiative, and to plunge into the silence of attentive receptivity where the text may reveal itself and read the reader.[29]

> [T]he stilling and letting-go characteristic [of contemplation] facilitates the liberation into and assumption of the different perspectives of the apophatic consciousness [deep mind], by yielding the hermeneutic initiative. In allowing itself to be read by the Transcendental Signified, the soul learns a new way of reading—*lectio Domini*—that allows it to escape, albeit fleetingly, from the play of absence and presence.[30]

What applies to the Christian applies in general to readers of every religious persuasion or none: attention to the other, whether God, a person, a text, a work of art, or creativity, is effected by the process described in the kenotic hymn. Belief, religious commitment, or lack of these are irrelevant, even though the following quotation is cast in religious terms:

> Our self-consciousness, coupled with our inventive rationality gives us the idea that we are little gods, each of us at the center of a little universe. If we cling to this illusory and anxious narrative, we become prey to manipulation, the push-me-pull-you of what other people think, of our status, our possessions, our fame or lack of it. This is the level of noise. But it is very frightening to let go of illusion, what *appears* to be our life, our "equality with God." Here the RSV's "grasped" is a far more appropriate translation than the NRSV's theologically misleading "exploited." We do have a shared nature with God, but it is the opposite of what appears and what we attempt to hold on to.
>
> To choose to enter silence, to let go of the illusion of power and control, is very like death. But it is precisely this passage that sets "free those who all their lives were held in slavery by the fear of death" (Heb 2:15). We must become willing slaves of a different sort, wholly given over to that silence where the observing I/eye is no longer present. This is faith, not propositional belief. [Again, the [en-Christing] process, the work of silence is not tied to religious faith.] Dread is appropriate: this is a "space for dangerous exploration and immense change."[31] This humbling, this letting go of our ideas and stereotypes stretches

---

29. This is but one example of the paradox of intention, discussed in Volume 1. See Shaw, *The Paradox of Intention*.

30. Gillespie and Ross, "The Apophatic Image," 56; bracketed comment mine.

31. Williams, Rowan, personal communication.

and opens us far beyond what we imagine our selves to be; it is a crucifixion indeed.

Thus we enter the "therefore" of the hymn, the limitless space of gift and potential.[32]

Roland Barthes describes the writerly process by which the author hopes to effect this shift in the reader, what he has called an "orgasmic text," which "dislocates the reader's historical, cultural and psychologi-cal assumptions, the consistency of his tastes, values and memories, and brings to a crisis his relation with language."[33]

It is in this "limitless space of gift and potential," entered coopera-tively by creator and reader, that the text or work of art or other person can begin to speak to us, to reveal itself to us. Then and only then is it possible to formulate a "theory" to try to express what has been revealed to us. "Fundamentally the method demands that we abandon the com-fortable noise of information-retrieval for the uncertainty of what the silence and the text may teach us."[34] Secular-minded scholars may object, but the effort to exercise too much control over interpretation is a recog-nized problem in philosophy. As Karmen MacKendrick notes:

> We still must use words; we still must draw out the questions that lie within philosophy. It is only that we have learned that we must use philosophy against itself, wrap our words around spaces without words, and leave them wordless, as if they could thus be kept, though we know that we lose them together with ourselves.[35]

What is true of texts is also true when interpreting other artistic endeavours:

> I evolved a way of looking at paintings which was massively time-consuming and deeply rewarding. For I came to recognize that it often took the first hour or so in front of a painting for stray associations or motivated misperceptions to settle down, and it was only then, with the same amount of time or more to spend looking at it, that the picture could be relied upon to disclose itself as it was.[36]

32. Ross, "Jesus in the Balance," 158–59; bracketed comments mine.

33. Gillespie and Ross, "The Apophatic Image," 56; Barthes, *The Pleasure of the Text*, 14.

34. Gillespie and Ross, "'With mekeness aske perseverantly'," 134.

35. MacKendrick, *Immemorial Silence*, 5.

36. Wollheim, *Painting as an Art*, 8. Julian Barnes also recognizes the problem:

It is but a short step from the empty space between the cherubim to Julian's paradoxical image of the empty space within the crown of thorns, which opens her text. This image is, as it were, a lens through which the reader/participant must pass (this is what she means by "comprehended"); it is also, as it were, a lens through which the divine engages the reader/participant. Later in the text, the thorns reveal themselves to be human beings. For Christ, humans are both a cause of suffering—his willing suffering with them[37]—and his crowning glory, his joy at their being offered a way out of the trap of suffering through beholding:

> . . . and therewith was comprehended and specified the Trinity with the incarnation and unite betwix God and man soule, with many faire sheweings of endless wisdome and teacheing of love, in which all the shewings that follow be grounded and onyd.[38]

What has been said by Steven Chase about the space between the cherubim in Richard of St. Victor's *Mystical Ark*[39]—a text unknown to Gillespie and myself at the time of writing of "The Apophatic Image" (1992)—applies to Julian's foundational image:

> The description of this emblem, with its apophatic centre surrounded by the signs of human suffering, characterizes the synthetic writing of so much of the text in the way it holds in tension conflicting perspectives. It is the ground on which all the showings are founded, but it encompasses them and unifies them. The Trinity is both comprehended and specified by it, suggesting a broad perspective and a minutely particular analysis. It exists in historical, linear time, but comprehends and circumscribes the whole of creation history. Its paradoxical resonance signifies the experience of humiliation for the sake of truth and love that lies at the heart of the Trinity and of the incarnation. It places a model of self-emptying humility as the cornerstone of the textual edifice, invoking the kenosis of Christ

---

"Bracque thought the ideal state would be reached when one said nothing at all in front of a painting. . . . But it is a rare picture that stuns, or argues, us into silence, and if one does, it is only a short time before we want to explain and understand the very silence into which we have been plunged." BBC4 June 23, 2015 from *Keeping an Eye Open: Essays on Art*, 8.

37. This is a reversal of Anselm's penal theory of the atonement.

38. Julian of Norwich, *A Revelation of Love*, 1.

39. Chase, *Angelic Wisdom*.

in his incarnation and passion . . . [Footnote 21: It is only in St John's Gospel that the crowning with thorns acquires a similar ironic prominence through the revelation of Jesus as Truth (John 18:33—19:5).][40]

We described the displacing activity necessary to entering attentive receptivity by means of apophatic images as follows:

> Apophatic images and apophatic surfaces contribute to this process by the effects they have on the ratiocinative and interpretative processes of the discursive mind. Like language, imagery exists in syntactical and grammatical patterns and acquires meaning through its position in the iconic repertoire. It operates a lexis of likeness and difference within a system of conventional signs. By denying the imagination the raw material for the kind of imagistic chain reactions so effectively described by the *Cloud*-author, an apophatic image or surface can allow the eyes of the soul to be focussed without interference from the fallen powers of the mind. They gesture toward the apophatic like the angels gesturing towards the imageless heart of the Holy of Holies.
>
> Such images and surfaces tend to the paradoxical. Water, wine, pearls, the moon, clouds, a flame, all partake of a play of light and darkness and offer neutral surfaces on which images can resolve and dissolve themselves. The coinherence of meaning or layers of meaning in a single image is a hallmark of the liminal signifiers of the apophatic. They defy or defer the lapse into linearity and monovalency that characterises most conventional interpretation and allow for the generation of productive paradoxes within the same signifier. The Middle English *Pearl* becomes an apophatic image for a range of spiritual truths that resonate together with incrementally synergistic force even though their host image has no necessary figural relationship to them. The pearl of Ephrem the Syrian, with its translucent opacity, becomes the gateway to new perception:
>
>> I saw in the pearl hidden places, that had no shadows,
>> for it is the Luminary's daughter,
>> in it types are eloquent
>> although they have no tongue;
>> symbols are uttered,
>> but without the help of lips
>> the silent lyre

40. Gillespie and Ross, "The Apophatic Image," 59.

though it has no sound, gives forth its song.[41]

Freed from earthly systems and signs, symbols are uttered without the help of lips. This is a communication that is above the mediation of language.

Apophatic images and surfaces are themselves non-figural but allow projection from within the viewer or perception derived from ineffable knowing. Moses' encounter with the burning bush is a classic apophatic image which allows the focussing of the imagination on a single image but which eschews representation of what it communicates. Similarly a candle flame offers a non-figural, non-linear and non-representational surface over which the mind can play and by which it may come to stillness. But even representational images can become springboards into the apophatic. Intense, unwavering attention to an image can causes it to lose its primary figural significance and to dissolve into constituent shapes, colours, patterns or textures. This commonplace deconstruction of the figural illustrates the metamorphosis of the figuratively allusive into the figurally elusive when the usual interpretative strategies are temporarily suspended.[42]

From these quotations it can be seen that one of the most important principles of reading texts such as Ephrem's and Julian's is that *all meanings are meant*. That is to say, when encountering apophatic images and similar strategies such as conflated subjects and objects, word-knots, deliberate ambiguity, self-subversion, hyperbole, and so forth (explained below), it is important to allow the multitude of meanings to resonate together without narrowing the interpretation to a single meaning. The failure of many modern translators and interpreters to allow this free play of resonances has resulted in texts that are flattened, texts that have lost most of their impact. That is to say, they have lost their ability to bypass the linear self-conscious mind to work directly at the level of deep mind. This failure to make translation as resonant as the original also makes texts such as the Bible, or *Beowulf*, or *The Cloud of Unknowing* extremely difficult to read, much less read aloud. Not only are resonances lost, but also the natural speech and breath patterns, which are an intrinsic part of the meaning of such texts.[43]

---

41. Hymns on Faith no. 81: "On the Pearl and its Symbols," in Brock, *The Luminous Eye*, 81. See the discussion by him in ibid., *passim*.

42. Gillespie and Ross, "The Apophatic Image," 56–57.

43. I am indebted to Vincent Gillespie and Daniel McCann for this insight.

Like the experience of childbirth that seems to inform so much of Julian's imagery in [the] early showings, her text has a rhythm, a pattern of movement. It has moments of great difficulty and density where meaning is intense and contracted; and it has moments of easier comprehension, relaxation, reflection and consolidation. These textual and spiritual contractions are the means by which the spiritual perception of Julian and her audience is dilated, making us open to new understanding, moving us closer to the moment of spiritual delivery, which may be deferred beyond the confines of the written text.[44]

I would now like to take a brief look at some of the other strategies that help to subvert the self-reflexive character of language and to bring the reader to attentive receptivity. The first has to do with the word "sodenly" in Julian's Long Text, in which she plays with time, perspective, conflation, and apophatic image. Chapter 4 begins, "In this sodenly I saw the rede blode treklyn downe fro under the garland . . ." [ch. 4, p. 5].

"In this sodenly" she perceives the blood trickling down from the freshly imposed crown of thorns. The opening of the chapter typifies our experience of Julian's syntactical virtuosity, for *sodenly* can be read here both as having a simple adverbial function (In this vision suddenly I saw [beheld]) and as functioning as the subject of the sentence (within this 'suddenly', I perceived the trickling blood). She signals the conflated time scale of her vision and its subsequent process of revelation by creating a multilayered sequence of showings and perceptions all happening in the apophatic landscape of her sudden instant. Through her use of insistent present participles she sustains us in a timeless beholding of the . . . context in which the historical moment is suspended.[45]

At this point it is worth repeating what was said above: "strategies such as conflated subjects and objects, word-knots, deliberate ambiguity, self-subversion, hyperbole, and so forth . . . allow the multitude of meanings to resonate together without narrowing the interpretation to a single meaning." Reading in this way is rather like free association. It should be also be noted again that these strategies not only overlap but coinhere.

44. Gillespie and Ross, "The Apophatic Image," 65–66.
45. Gillespie and Ross, "The Apophatic Image," 61.

Thus, in the example of "sodenly" we see conflation, altered time, apophatic image, and deliberate ambiguity working in a single movement.

The orgasmic "sodenly" is immediately followed by conception: "Having been delivered of the world, she immediately *conceives* that Christ is showing her this image without any 'mene'" [ch. 4, p. 5]. It is worth quoting footnote 28 in full, because it describes word-knots and the polysemous aspects of "mene":

> Julian's lexical exploration of the word *mene*, as a noun, adjective, and verb, is one of the most dazzling illustrations of her verbal dexterity in creating semantic clusters or "word-knots." [The term is extrapolated from the medieval image of love-knots.] Here she seems to imply that the showing was without speech and without intermediary. The nominal senses of *mene* include: sexual intercourse; fellowship; a companion; a course of action, method or way; an intermediary or negotiator; an agent or instrument; an intermediate state; something uniting extremes; mediation or help; argument, reason, or discussion. Adjectivally it can mean "partaking of the qualities or characteristics of two extremes." As a verb it has the senses of: to intend to convey something; to signify; to say or express something; to remember something; to advise, admonish, or urge somebody to do something. It can also have the sense of: to complain; to cry out for help; to pity, sympathise with, or condole with somebody. A further adjectival set of senses coheres around notions of lowness, inferiority, and smallness which resonates with Julian's sense of humble self-emptying. (*MED*, sv *mene*, n.; *menen*, v.). Julian's exploitation of the polysemousness of this word means that it becomes the meeting place for many of her key ideas, perceptions, responses, and expressions.

All meanings are meant. Word-knots are but one of the strategies by which she does theology:

> Typically she takes a nucleus word and winds around it strands of homonyms, grammatical variants, near-puns and half-rhymes that constitute the genetic code of her theology. The lexical and theological relationships that such "word-knots" generate are both playful and profound, . . . they [reveal] themselves[46] most fully . . . in the interaction between text, reflective silence, and speculative gropings for understanding.[47]

46. Gillespie and Ross, "'With Mekeness . . .'"135.

47. Gillespie and Ross, "The Apophatic Image," 61–62.

Immediately after the showing of the bleeding head, there is another "sodenly": "sodenly the Trinite fulfilled the herte most of ioy" [ch. 4, p. 6].

> Again this is not a process but an instantaneous perception; in effect another moment of conception. The lack of *means*, the suspension of the usual convention of interpretation, allows her to impact the joy of the Trinity onto the grief and humiliation of the crowning with thorns. This allows the physical paradox of the mocked kingship of Christ to resonate with its full theological force in a manner unusual in late medieval Passion narratives.
>
> Julian's verbal reaction to the shewing—*Benedicte domine*—is said "for reverence in my meneing" because her rational powers are astonished: ". . . for wonder and marvel . . . that he that is so reverend and dredfull will be so homely with a synfull creature liveing in wretched flesh."[48] Again the syntactical looseness (which so annoyed Colledge and Walsh) is revealed as a functional part of Julian's theology of immanence. Christ is *reverend* and *dredfull* (in both senses), but also *homely*: the nature of the paradox is manifest in the final clause "liveing in wretched flesh . . . ," the antecedent for which can be both Julian and Christ. His homeliness with his creatures extends to occupying the same syntactical space as them. Her *conceiving* of the significance of the shewing is acted out by the way the spirit of God fills her syntax and occupies her subclauses in a grammatical parody of the Incarnation. Her puzzlement is overcome by her reverence as she is led into the annunciation of truths whose enunciation defies language.
>
> This conception of Christ's meaning without means, analogous to the Incarnation without physical intermediary, is only possible because she has moved to a position of true *compassion* with Christ. . . . Christ's willingness for death becomes real for her at what she believes is the moment of her own death, the labour pains of which she reclaims as an act of willed self-emptying . . . .[49]

But there are more meanings here. One of them continues to spin a "theologically subtle" thread of the Annunciation:

---

48. Ibid. Note that the "wretched flesh" "conflates Christ in the incarnation, the Virgin Mary, Julian, and (by implication) the reader, a theological effect achieved by word order alone." Gillespie and Ross, "With mekeness aske perseverantly,'" 126–41.

49. Gillespie and Ross, "The Apophatic Image," 62–63.

We see Mary "wan she conceived with child," echoing and rever-
berating against Julian's own conceiving of her revelation [and
her death, and Christ's, and the joy of the Trinity; we might even
say she is pregnant with all the meanings]. We see her wisdom
and truth: "wherein I understood the reverend beholding that
she beheld hir God and maker, mervelyng with greate reverence
that he would be borne of hir that was a simple creature of his
makeyng" [ch. 4, p. 6].

Julian's syntactical openness again allows theology to take
place within the grammatical interstices of the sentence. When
we ask who is 'mervelyng with greate reverence' at this scene, we
realise that it must be *both* Mary and Julian [not to mention the
reader!] Their responses are twinned just as their vocabulary of
reverent dread at God's homeliness with creatures has also been
subliminally twinned. Mary's meekness in acquiescing (Lo me,
God's handmayd) is a scriptural analogue (and a *post hoc* vali-
dation) of Julian's earlier *Benedicite domine*. Moreover, Mary's
beholding of God ushers in a major theme of later revelations;
how God is to be perceived and how that perception is to be
articulated. *Beholding* is a key term in Julian's apophatic vocabulary, signalling not an analytical, critical or interpretative seeing,
but rather a still and mutual enjoyment of and exchange of being
between God and the soul.[50]

We might also note that Julian's astonishing text coupled with her
use of the word "behold" or "beholding" has also conceived in the reader
a new way of reading and that the purpose of her text is to deliver her
"even Christian" into the same showings of love.

Julian is not only the apostle of beholding, but also a master of
paradox. She understands, for example, that to "clevyn to the goodnes of
God"[51] means the complete detachment (noughting) that is bound up in
the word-knot of *mene* and is the strand of another word-knot tied with
the threads of various levels of knowing, nothing, no-thing, and effacement (nowted).[52]

The discomfort of our earlier textual labours is rewarded with
images of nurturing reassurance that invoke the registers of ma-
ternal and sexual love: "He is our clotheing that for love wrap-
pith us [halseth] us and all beclosyth us for tender love" [ch.
5, p. 7]. We cannot rest until we are "beclosyd" in God [which

---

50. Ibid., 64; brackets mine.
51. Julian of Norwich, *A Revelation of Love*, 7.
52. Gillespie and Ross, "The Apophatic Image," 65.

means complete openness, to free-fall in the love of God, as it were], but this is only [possible] by our approaching him "nakidly and plainly and homely."[53] . . . This passover, or death to the world liberates us from the enclosure of worldly thought and into the enclosing and clothing love of God [which shields us from images and conjectures]. Her language here is finessing the liturgy of monastic clothing and of the enclosure of hermits and anchoresses to offer, in effect, a theology of enclosure for all Christians.[54]

The next strategy is effacement by inversion:

> But with her characteristic suspicion of analogy, she moves quickly to preempt crude schematization. . . . Having used the analogy of concentric layers to emphasize the enfolding love of God, she inverts this initial perspective of enclosure, liberating us into the boundless wholeness of God by the peripeteia [reversal] of our expectations and the denial of the similitude ("without any likenes" [ch. 6, p. 9]).[55]

An effacement strategy applies to her most famous image, that of the hazelnut: there isn't one; it vanishes before it is established; it is only a gesture indicating size, which she immediately effaces; and, for even greater emphasis, follows this effacement with another inversion of perspective.

> In this same time our lord shewed to me a ghostly sight of his homely loveing. I saw that he is to us everything that is good and comfortable for us. He is our clotheing that for love wrappith us [halseth] us and all beclosyth us for tender love that he may never leave us, being to us althing that is gode. Also in this he shewed a little thing, the *quantitye* of an hesil nutt in the palme of my hand; and it was as round as a balle.

Simultaneously we are being offered an image which does not exist. What Julian sees is not a hazelnut but an unspecified thing, about the size of a hazelnut if it were in the palm of her hand (which it is not), and as round as a ball . . . its true properties, as perceived by Julian, are *not* its materiality or referentiality but rather aspects of God's relationship to it.

---

53. Ibid.
54. Ibid., 66.
55. Ibid., 64; bracketed comments mine.

> I lokid thereupon with eye of my understondyng and thowte: "What may this be?" And it was generally answered thus: "It is all that is made." I mervellid how it might lesten, for methowte it might suddenly have fallen to nowte for littil. And I was answered in my understondyng: "It lesteth and ever shall, for God loveth it; and so allthing hath the being be the love of God." In this littil thing I saw iii properties: the first is that God made it, the second is that God loveth it, the iiid, that God keepith it.[56]

She has reversed perspective from her own, limited point of view to God's infinite perspective, and then goes on to short-circuit any attempt by the reader to schematize:

> [The hazelnut] has being in our minds only as a function of God's creative and sustaining love. She even refuses to attribute these powers to the particular persons of the Trinity. So we are left with an effaced image of creation held in being by a power whose trinitarian functions are denied exact demarcation in terms of earthly activity or theological convention. Julian again balances her description on the brink of the apophatic.[57]

She goes on in the early part of chapter 6[58] to add yet another resonance to the word *mene*, tied closely to this strategy of effacement:

> Her critique of human *means* [for the present age the cult of manufactured "experience"] in devotion is hard hitting. Most are "to litil and not full worshippe to God." She includes many of the common objects of affective devotion and prayer: his holy flesh, pretious blood, passion, death and wounds, his mother, the cross and saints. These human and earthbound devotions are all aspects and functions of the divine goodness [but] they are too often seen as ends in themselves, not as proper means to the apprehension of the deity, of cleaving to him with the love to which we must aspire. "The chiefe and principal mene is the blissid kind that he took of the mayd"[59] [ch. 6, p. 9], [that is to say, our shared nature with God]. To come to him nakedly, plainly

---

56. Julian of Norwich, *A Revelation of Love*, 7.

57. Gillespie and Ross, "The Apophatic Image," 67.

58. Julian of Norwich, *A Revelation of Love*, 8.

59. Gillespie and Ross, "The Apophatic Image," 68, note 40: Here she is punning on the role of Christ as intercessor, intermediary, and companion, as well as alluding to the humanity of Christ as a *mene* state, both in its lowness and its function as a link (I am the way . . . (or means)) between humanity and God. Once again, Jesus was a person; Christ is a process.

and homely may require the shedding of artificial means and
techniques. By passing over from earthly means we are enabled
to apprehend something of the love of God, which "overpassyth
the knoweing of all creatures."[60]

It is not a question of regarding language as an enemy, any more than self-conscious knowing: quite the reverse. Language and silence, words and gestures, self-consciousness and deep mind, must inform one another.

> But her careful and circumspect criticism of "the custome of our
> praying" [ch. 6, p. 8] is not founded on a despairing silence. Her
> prayer at the end of chapter 5 is based on her psychology of hu-
> man need expressed in chapter 6. Our words "arn full lovesome
> to the soule" [ch. 5, p. 7] and offer verbal formulae that allow us
> to enact a kenotic gesture towards the ineffable will of God. In-
> deed they "full nere touchen the will of God and his goodness"
> [ch. 5, p. 7]. The groping into the unsayable, itself stimulated by
> the touching of the Holy Spirit, will be comprehended by the
> goodness of God. The gesture is of humility not of control. God's
> comprehension of us encloses us as well as understands us.

There are echoes here again of the opening and grounding image of the text: the emblem of the crown of thorns with an apophatic center. In this case, the words are the thorns in the crown, both flawed and glorious; stepping into the apophatic centre, as it were, is the equivalent of God's clothing/enclosing us with his comprehension, and supporting us with his understanding.

> God is able to read us, no matter how flawed the text, and we
> seek to read God by allowing God to read us: this is the essence
> of *lectio Domini.*
>
> *lectio Divina*
>
> Absence and lack, the sense of figural emptiness that Julian
> generates in these early chapters produces the attentive silence
> of beholding necessary for transfigured perception. . . . Signs are
> not rejected or despised; they are exalted by being transfigured.
> The emptiness of the ineffable [as distinct from the vacuity of
> sin] and the apophatic becomes occupied, filled, and fulfilled
> "in fullhede of joy" [ch. 6, p. 9] (another word-knot) by the love
> of God. "Beholding and lovyng of the maker" [ch. 6, p. 10] is
> transactional: God and the soul behold and love each other.
>   Her beholding allows her to see from God's perspective (as
> one who shared God's meaning); her beholding allows her to see
> the irreduceable unity of the showing (I beheld it all in one, by

---

60. Gillespie and Ross, "The Apophatic Image," 67–68; bracketed comments mine.

means of God's showing); and she beholds it as someone who
has herself become a means of showing, a signifier for those
who, she expects, will survive her:

> And that I say of me I sey in the person of my even christen,
> for I am lernyd in the gostly showing of our lord God that
> he menyth so. [ch. 8, p. 13].

God means her to be the means of communicating to all
Christians. This is how God "menyth" or speaks: she becomes
the word spoken by God.[61]

These strategies are taken to another level in the second revelation.
It is both more abstract and yet does not lose its grounding or context.
Instead,

> She embarks on a tangential meditation on the changing colour
> of Christ's face, typically welding the static and the kinetic, the
> spatial and the linear. The blood closes over the face, veiling it
> from view behind an apophatic surface. . . .
>
> This is an important moment of *impasse* for Julian's percep-
> tion of the imagery of her showings. She wishes to see more
> clearly with her bodily sight, but the image is "derke"—both in
> the sense of lacking illumination and in the cognate sense of
> enigmatic. She is unwilling to relinquish control of the signi-
> fication of her vision. Her reliance on bodily sight is answered
> in her reason [self-consciousness]—the seat of this controlling
> impulse:
>
>> If God wil shew thee more, he shal be thy light. Thee nedith
>> none but him. [ch. 10, p.15].
>
> God will be the means of the showing and will provide the
> means by which she should receive and respond to it. God again
> has the initiative in the hermeneutics of the texts. She sees him
> but seeks him, recognising that we are now blind and unwise.
> She has him but wants him; the play of absence and presence
> flickers between her bodily sight and her sense of something
> more beyond for which she longs, but which she is prevented
> from seeing by the veil of blood and by her own blindness and
> lack of wisdom (a wisdom associated with the self-emptying of
> Mary in the first showing.[62]

---

61. Ibid., 68–69.
62. Ibid., 69–70.

method

This requirement to let go trying to control the interpretation of the text cannot be emphasized strongly enough. While we may be aware of various strategies that such a text as Julian's might employ, reading with these in the back of one's mind is not a game of "I spy with my little eye." Rather, one must sit with the text, inhabit the text, and allow the text to have the hermeneutic initiative. While it is possible to point to these strategies, they will inevitably be used in ways unique to each text and in the end they efface themselves. Reading such texts *requires time, reflection, attentive receptivity*, the very modes of perception that Julian is trying to teach her readers. Her text is perhaps unique in that its content simultaneously teaches an explicit method of reading. Other texts, such as that of the Pseudo-Dionysius and Richard of St. Victor teach similar content, but the method is implicit.

The method of our seeing continues both through grammar and through more paradox. First the grammar:

> he will be sene and he wil be sowte; he wil be abdyn and he
> wil be trosted [ch. 10, p. 15].

> Again her grammatical skills allow a density of reference. The
> future tenses imply an idealised future perfect; *will* as a modal
> auxiliary implies the determination of God to reveal himself to
> his creatures; and the mood allows a sense of God tolerating his
> creatures' feeble attempts to conform themselves to his will.

And now the paradox, perhaps the ultimate paradox:

> like as we were like made to the Trinite in our first makyng,
> our maker would that we should be like Iesus Christe our
> saviour in hevyn without ende, be the vertue of our geyn-
> making. [Ch. 10, p. 16]

> Our *geynmaking* must be achieved by a renewal or uncovering
> of the image and likeness of God in our soul.
> Christ is so determined that we should see him that in the
> Incarnation and Passion *he uses our sins . . . as the means of
> renewing that image.*[63]

This sentence recalls one of the most famous quotations from this text: "sin is behoovly." We *need* our sins, in order to make us realize our little-ness and our need, and through this paradox our wounds, mirroring those of Christ, are glorified.

---

63. Ibid., 71; italics mine.

> Sin is turned to our advantage by the emptying humility of
> the passion. . . . [S]in clouds true sight[;] . . . God redeems it
> and forces it to be a *means* of seeing God clearly. The blood is
> wiped from Christ's eyes and his true beauty shines out for us to
> contemplate in our ghostly sight. Christ has used the means of
> imagery to draw us into the apophatic. . . .
>
> Beyond the veil of paradox, we behold God just as God eter-
> nally beholds us. This mutual beholding restores the image that
> gives us clearness of sight . . . .[64]

Again, the emphasis is on the hermeneutic initiative that is God's through
images that efface themselves:

> Faith seeking understanding manifests itself here by a seeking
> into images to find a way of beholding God; a new grammar of
> spiritual imagery. Only the Transcendental Signified can reveal
> that grammar: "how a soule shall have him in his beholdyng he
> shall teche himself" [ch. 10, p.16]. The yearning of the soul for
> blissful sight always invites God with the words of Mary: *Ecce
> ancilla domini*. Seeking is the *Ecce* of the soul, a self-emptying in
> readiness for the Holy Spirit's annunciation of new meaning.[65]

But Julian takes care that we do not fall into a categorization of the
modes of seeing, that the way to beholding is not formulaic. She goes to
great lengths to ensure that her readers are not trapped in the prison of
their own expectations. Chapter 11 begins

> And after this I saw God in a poynte, that is to sey, in myn
> vnderstondyng, be which sight I saw that he is in all things.
> [p. 17].
>
> The sense of this highly elliptical passage has preoccupied com-
> mentators from the time of the Paris manuscript onwards. Syn-
> tactically and lexically she is going to considerable lengths to
> signal that the ground of this showing . . . defies simple categori-
> sation. She gives no indication whether this is a bodily sight,
> word formed in her understanding, or ghostly sight (indeed she
> may mean that all three modes are simultaneously present in
> all the showings when they are fully perceived and realized).
> God in a point may be deliberately enigmatic: it is certainly
> non-figural and non-referential. It is apophatic in that one can
> imagine what she means without being able to represent it in
> terms of imagery. Her qualification of the main clause—"that

64. Ibid., 71.
65. Ibid., 71–72.

is to sey"—purports to offer clarification but ushers in further complexity. "In myn vnderstondyng" can relate adverbially to *saw* (I saw in my understanding). It can also stand in apposition to the object of the main clause: I saw God in a point, that is to say in my understanding. This would reinforce her developing awareness of God's indwelling and immanence. If *point* also means an instant of time (like the *sodenly* of her first showing), then she is further effacing the referential towards a moment of blissful sapiential *jouissance*. Certainly her attempt to capture her response to it reverberates with complexity and an unwillingness to affix simple psychological labels . . . .

Julian's play between discursive (self-conscious mind) and intuitive (deep mind) ways of knowing in her discussion of sin echoes that of presence and absence.

By conflating affective and intellective modes of perception she tries to open up in the reader's experience some sense of her own experience. [Her] use of apophatic paradox is a response to her avowed inability to represent the ghostly sight "as hopinly ne as fully as I wolde" [ch. 9, p. 14]. . . . [S]in is denied materiality or representation. She does not see sin and she sees no-sin: both her perceptions are, of course, perceptions of God, and profoundly apophatic answers to her discursive question "What is synne?" [ch. 11, p. 17]. The slippage of the prose away from referentiality invites her to yield up ratiocinative curiosity and the hermeneutical initiative, and return to a state of beholding.

This is a key moment in the text, and a particularly dangerous one, for she is challenging the late medieval emphasis on sin by which the institution held people in thrall, and kept them captive in an endless cycle of guilt and forgiveness, confused by the noise of doctrine and prevented from beholding. The implication here is that sin has no substance (she echoes the orthodox teaching of her day), and whatever suffering sin causes can be healed by seeking to the beholding—beholding *is* our substance and our sharing in joy, the density of God's glory—not by endless repetition of words (or penances), be they words of contrition or words of doctrine. A solipsistic fretting about sin in general or one's own sin in particular is like picking at a scab to the degree that the wound remains open and subject to infection. Instead, contrite turning to seek into the beholding is the best, and indeed the only, remedy. This insight will later be echoed in the parable of the lord and the servant.

This turning requires a shift from the false beholding of "the blind demyng of man" to the true beholding of the "faire swete demyng of God" [ch.11, p. 18]. The complacent beholding of her own logical processes is more difficult and less satisfying than the message of God's benevolent immanence: "How should anything be amysse?" [ch. 11, p. 19] Indeed, Julian recognises the folly of her earlier *questio* on sin and the subsequent one-sided *disputatio* when she concludes the showing with an amused parody of the language of the schools.

> Thus mightily, wisely, and lovinly was the soul examynyd in this vision. Then saw I sothly that me behovyd nedis to assenten with gret reverens, enioyand in God. [ch. 11, p. 19].[66]

Her extended contemplation of the Passion conflates several perspectives, radically departing from convention.

> As her contemplation of the Passion deepens and unfolds, Julian comes to understand that the contrition and compassion of her beholding of Christ's "herd peyne" [ch. 21, p. 30] is only one mode of beholding. In the ninth revelation she will be shown two more perspectives: that the love that made him suffer surpasses all his pains; and the "ioy and the blis that make hym to lekyn it" [ch. 23, p. 33]. In fact, all three perspectives are immanent in the earlier showings and gradually begin to emerge with increasing clarity as her "avisement" develops. But the eighth showing is the last to be grounded on the suffering and death of Christ. Labouring through his grief and pain, she reinforces and deepens her understanding of the mutual self-emptying involved in true compassion:

> > Thus was our lord Iesus nawted for us, and we stond al in this manner nowtid with hym; and shall done til we come to his blisse . . . [ch. 18, p. 28].

The pain of sin and the torment of temptation are left behind in our self-emptying that mirrors and coinheres with Christ's. And as we behold him even as Julian did, we see that he has "chongyd his blissful chere"; even so is our own chere chongyd. Thus:

> In a further paradox, noughting is the route to oneing. This gives her the strength to resist the temptation to look away from the Cross which comes as a "profir in my reason as it had be friendly . . ." [ch. 19, p. 28]. This temptation, masquerading as a

66. Ibid., 75.

reasonable development of her spiritual sight, seeks to lure her into a false apophatic. Its appearance in her reason is significant as it seeks to reintroduce the analysis, temporality and linearity that Julian has learned to suspend . . . .[67]

It cannot be too strongly emphasized that even as there is a false emptiness—the vacuity of sin—there is also a false apophatic. To willfully change her gaze would be once again to seize the initiative and attempt hermeneutic control; to look away from the image that is leading her into the apophatic would be an implicit denial of the incarnation and a rejection of the immanence and hermeneutical grace through beholding that she is being given.

> Loke up to hevyn to his Fader. [ch. 19, p. 28]

> Heaven is physically distant, materially visible and occupied by a Father who is hierarchically superior and distinct from the Son. This is contrary to the enfolding and unitary dynamic of her showings.
> Julian recognizes, however, that the image of the crucified Christ, resonant as a new kind of signifier, offers no hindrance to her apophatic beholding and is, indeed, the guarantee of her spiritual well-being:

> > And then I saw wele with the feyth that I felte that ther was nothyn betwix the crosse and hevyn that might have desesyd me [ch 19, p.28].

Julian understands that the paradoxical image of the humanity of Christ—already becoming a vexed topic in her day—is the motivation and doorway for her own self-emptying beyond all images; the image will efface itself. She understands that seeking to beholding uses everything and anything ready to hand as long as one yields the desire for control and manipulation. Beholding cannot be forced: it can only be welcomed.

> Scorning the premisses of the offer, she reasserts her earlier desire "that I be so festined to him that there is right nowte that is made betwix my God and me" [ch. 5, p. 7]. She prefers to cleave to Christ, refusing to reclaim the initiative and happy to wait for him to unbind her into eternal bliss . . . .[68]

Christ's change of cheer (ch. 21, p. 31) effaces the last of her preoccupation with sin and death. It also emphasizes the earlier paradox that through

67. Ibid., 76.
68. Ibid., 76.

embracing our sin and pain we are healed and brought to joy. There is an echo here of John 16:20, ". . . your sorrow shall be turned into joy." There is also an echo of Jesus' words to the "good thief" in Luke 23:43: "Today you shall be with me in paradise," which is sometimes translated, "Even now [as we hang here on these crosses] you are with me in paradise."

> Physiological necessity and narrative logic have [led] her to attempt to extrapolate the "shewyng of the end." But as so often before, the divine logic is unpredictable and unreadable. The *sudden* change of cheer changes hers, "and I was as glad and as mery as it was possible" [ch.21, p. 31]. The question that forms in her mind ("Where is now ony poynt of the peyne or thin agreefe?") triggers a passover experience of overpassing understanding:

> > I understode that we be now in our lord's menyng in his crosse with hym in our peynys and our passion, deyng, and we wilfully abydyng in the same cross with his helpe and his grace into the last poynte, sodenly he shal chonge his chere to us, and we shal be with hym in hevyn. [ch. 21, p. 31][69]

> She inhabits the bliss of his meaning here in a new and profound sense. Our pains, passion and death (to ourselves, to the world, to the flesh, and to the devil) help us to share in his cross and to see from the divine perspective. The undoing of the word-knot around *means* is just the unbinding that Julian has longed for. God's meaning possesses her, and she sees clearly her role as the means by which the kenotic paradigm can be displayed through the transfigured means of earthly language.

> Julian draws together the accumulated resonances and overtones of the preceding revelations and discharges them in a blaze of apophatic glory:

> > We willfully abydyng in the same cross with his helpe and his grace into the last poynte, sodenly he shall chonge his chere to us, and we shal be with hymn in hevyn. [ch. 21, p. 31]

> The extraordinary power of this passover derives partly from the fact that almost every word has been explored, ruminated,

---

69. Note 50: "This episode needs to be read in conjunction with chapter 13, when she sees God scorning the malice of the devil, and learns that this is the appropriate response. *Scorn* in Julian's day also means *ignore*: the way to deal with sin is to ignore it. As sin has no substance, it seeks attention to give it the illusion of substance, and the best way to fight it is to turn away from it to behold."

and potentiated in the preceding chapters. The "desese" and "travel" of our earthly labouring are a function of our "frelete" [p. 31] and our fettering into the "blind demyng" [ch. 11, p. 18] of the human perspective. But Christ's redemptive power ultimately transfigures us into a "hey endles knowing in God" [ch. 21, p. 31] by working through the linear temporal world in showing us his "time of passion" [ch. 21, p. 31]. His meaning (his self-humbling, his passion, his love, his intention, his intercession, his incarnation) opens the door to the bliss of heaven. His meaning is eternal; his means are temporal. Our wilful abiding, the paradox of intention and self-emptying, of noughting and knowing, will lead us finally to know and to become what he means:[70]

> Betwix that one and the other shall be no tyme, and than shal al be browte to ioy. [ch. 21, p. 31]

Even in the face of all this analysis, the reader should not think that it is possible to "comprehend" Julian's text or any other text of this ilk. Every time I re-read the Long Text, I find something new. It is inexhaustible. But I hope this unpacking of "the apophatic image" has at least shown why Julian's and similar texts need to be read in a polysemous way. The tropes described above are everywhere in the texts that etch themselves in our memories, and such texts and our reading of them will be all the richer if we yield the hermeneutic initiative and allow the texts to read themselves to us.

I would like now to return briefly to the poem on the pearl by Ephrem the Syrian (fourth century, verse 6 of the hymn cited above), as it illustrates how apophatic images help to move the mind from the discursive into the liminal and so into beholding, and also how they raise an important theological question.[71]

> 2. I placed it [the pearl] . . . in the palm of my hand
> in order to contemplate it. I turned to look at it
> from one side, but It had facets
> on every side. So it is with enquiry into the Son:
> it is something unattainable, for He is entirely light.

---

70. Gillespie and Ross, "The Apophatic Image," 76–77.

71. I am indebted to Sebastian Brock for insights into Ephrem. See Brock, *The Luminous Eye*.

3. In the luminosity of the pearl I saw the Luminous One
who cannot be perturbed. In its purity
is a wonderful symbol—the Body of our Lord,
utterly unsullied. In the undivided nature of the pearl
I beheld Truth, which is not divided.

6. I beheld within it hidden chambers that had no shadows,
for it is the daughter of the luminary. In it types are eloquent,
though they have no tongue; symbols are uttered
without the help of lips. The silent lyre,
though it has no sound, gives forth its songs.

12. The waves of the Son are full of benefits,
as well as harm. Have you not observed
how the waves of the sea, when a boat contends against them
breaks it up, but if the boat yields
without resisting, then it is saved.

15. Enquiry is joined in contest with Thanksgiving:
which will win? Praise rises up, like incense,
—and so does prying enquiry, both from the same tongue.
Which will God listen to? Prying and prayer come from a single
mouth. Which will he hear?

Ephrem's poems are full of biblical, liturgical, theological, and psychological allusions and plays on words and symbols. For example, the Syriac word for the consecrated eucharistic host is the same as the Syriac word for pearl, and, along with baptism, the eucharist is rich with bridal imagery (the Syriac words for soul and the Holy Spirit are feminine). In Ephrem's culture, pearls were thought to be created when lightning struck the sea and entered the oyster's shell. This process linked heaven and earth, and so the pearl became a symbol of the incarnation. *Symbols for Ephrem were not separated from what they symbolized.* Rather, they partook of the essence of what they symbolized, thus the power of the pearl symbolizing the Eucharist.

But leaving aside these insights into the significance of the pearl, I am more concerned with the way this poem expresses the two aspects of knowing and exposes the importance of not seeking to define and reify the insights and knowledge of deep mind. Ephrem hated definition; he felt strongly that the discursive mind should not put boundaries around the mysteries that could only be known apophatically, such as the incarnation—thus his fondness for paradox and typology. In the poem, the narrator tries to look at only one side of the pearl in a linear way, with his discursive mind. But the pearl is faceted—what we would call a baroque pearl—and even with facets it is a uniformly luminous surface; it is an apophatic image; it can be looked at appropriately only with the deep mind. Like the Son of God, the pearl is "entirely light." Similarly, it is both pure and unperturbed, symbolizing "Body of the Lord." In its unity it represents the unity of truth, of which we can only ever know fragments. It has "hidden chambers that had no shadows"; "types are eloquent, though they have no tongue, symbols are uttered without the help of lips"—there is an echo of Psalm 19 here: "though they [the heavens] have neither words nor language, yet is their sound gone out into all the world, and their words to the ends of the earth." The lyre is silent but gives forth its songs—harps are tightly strung and even when no one is playing them, they seem to be vibrating with music. For Ephrem, as for Pseudo-Denys and Maximus the Confessor who came after him, the highest praise and understanding of God were to be found in silence.

But then Ephrem turns to the crux of the question to which all these types ultimately refer, a question that haunted the Middle Ages, and haunts us still: prying or praying; discursive knowledge or beholding. It is not that Ephrem is anti-intellectual. Rather, he knows that there are some kinds of knowledge suited to discursive reasoning and some kinds of knowledge that can be understood only through typology and paradox, which are the apophatic gates to beholding.[72]

As we saw in the first volume of this book, it is not a question of either/or but of training the self-conscious and discursive mind to open to what the deep mind is offering, and then to yield the work it does back to the deep mind for further insight. It is a question of *appropriateness* and *balance*.

———•◦•———

The same preoccupation with two ways of knowing occurs among indigenous peoples. Here are some extracts from *Spirit of Eagle Rock: A Native American Cultural and Geologic Interpretation of Eagle Rock* by Coyote

---

72. F. Edward Cranz, in the epigraph to his book *Nicolas of Cusa and the Renaissance*, writes: ". . . maybe we should consider carefully whether in our secular context we can safely eliminate the beyond in our thinking. After all, Proclus and Cusanus are convinced from very different perspectives that without the beyond nothing could exist, without the beyond nothing could be thought, and without the beyond nothing could be said. It is perhaps true: *De te fabula est?*

Short. Short is a professional Geologist of the Paiute and Modoc Tribes and a maker of ceremonies; her heritage is half Paiute and half French.

Having no written language, the Boise Valley tribes used and extensive and highly developed language of stone to store and communicate the information necessary to support a sophisticated culture for many thousands of years.

In their versatility, stones can represent any type of knowledge: a memory, an event, a duty, a metaphor, a picture, a purpose, or a prayer. A language based on stone is economical while profoundly articulate as it allows knowledge to remain larger than words, *keeping the idea and the object as one.* [Italics mine.]

Native Americans possess the drive to clarify ideas and keep them *pure, direct, and consistent.* [Italics mine.] A language of stone supports this by accommodating the storage of *concentrated knowledge*—knowledge undiluted by words and interpretation. [Underscore mine.] And, by involving the individual directly, through tactile feedback to retrieve the stored information, high fidelity of the original idea is contained.

A language of stone perfectly addresses the responsibility and obligation felt by Native Americans to be free to speak to The Creator and the unknown, and to acknowledge, trust, and know that all is not contained in human power.[73]

A raven is a coyote with wings.[74] Since they can fly, the raven can see the big picture. Making a stone in the shape of a raven is a request for insight and powers of seeing beyond visual sense.[75]

To Native Americans, ceremony is kinaesthetic prayer—prayer in motion. It is well understood by Native Americans that the body can absorb an event and remember better than can the mind, which explains the active, physical nature of ceremony.

Ceremony is a way to resonate with The Creator—to connect with spiritual ideals and make them real in our lives. It is a way to take time to process events, to remember, to see principles in real time, to recapture the subtle essence of existence in a pure state.[76]

---

73. Coyte Short, *Spirit of Eagle Rock*, 16.

74. Coyote is a trickster and wisdom figure in many Native American cultures.

75. Ibid., 28.

76. Ibid., 30.

Ceremonies mark time and significant events in the lives of the people and acknowledge that our identity is linked to the land we live on.[77]

———◆———

There is another problem with reading texts that I would like to highlight before ending this chapter, and that is the failure of many readers *to pay attention to what the author is actually saying*. Related to this problem is that of slavishly following scholarly convention and language. In this concluding section, I will use Pseudo-Dionysius to illustrate what I mean.[78] The point here is to sketch out a problem, not to answer the questions that are raised.

For example, while reading Golitzin's interesting book *Mystagogy*,[79] it seemed to me that what is usually translated as "hierarchy" (whether celestial or ecclesiastical) in Pseudo-Denys would better be translated as "taxonomy." First of all, it is clear that Pseudo-Denys eschews elitism. Progress through the stages comes about only by a greater capacity for self-emptying, not by accumulating power and control. That which is most like God in us is our mind's ability to transcend itself.[80] This is perhaps why Pseudo-Denys discusses wisdom immediately after ecstasy in the *Divine Names*.[81] What he is describing is not a difference in value or power or any of the things by which we commonly think of church hierarchy, but rather the uniqueness of each creature to fulfil its *logos*, its reality, in God.

There might be a very loose analogy with evolution: for example, a range of creatures from single-cell animals to animals with complex eyes have relationship to the light. One is not "better" than the other; the strategies for a relationship of light differ. But each is uniquely evolved to its own perfection. The analogy breaks down in that human beings have the potential to enlarge their capacity; it is not biologically determined.

In human terms, each level of the hierarchy/taxonomy is supposed to enlighten the one beneath so that in the end the hierarchy effaces itself. The

77. Ibid., 31.

78. Pseudo-Denys also speaks of the "hidden mind" CH145C, *Pseudo-Dionysius*, 108.

79. Golitzin, *Mystagogy, passim*.

80. René Roques' introduction in Luibheid and Rorem, *Pseudo-Dionysius*, 6. DN 592C–592D.

81. Luibheid and Rorem, *Pseudo-Dionysius*, 106–10.

continual references to moving from multiplicity to simplicity could easily be observations of how the mind works. For example, in CH 145B he refers to the deep mind: "Keep these holy truths a secret in your hidden mind. Guard their unity safe from the multiplicity of what is profane . . . ."

This movement—and Pseudo-Denys corpus is characterized by movement—possibly is grounded in Pseudo-Deny's affinity for the Gospel of John where the disciples' relationship to Jesus changes from being servants to friends. In the event, there appears to be an *anti*-hierarchical intent. The problem is that early on the Dionysian texts were latched onto to justify institutional hierarchies in the real world, without asking the questions that might have led to different conclusions, such as the possibility that Pseudo-Denys could be writing—especially in terms of the ecclesiastical hierarchy—gentle satire. His playfulness, his exaggerated picture of idealized ecclesiastical hierarchy in an age when actual hierarchies were anything but ideal, suggests this, as does Letter 8, which is highly critical, and also his sardonic remarks about people who attempt to raise themselves to priesthood by means of secondary resources instead of praxis.[82] And as individual illumination is linked with degrees of hierarchy, it is possible to have a layperson at the highest degree, even though he/she is not ordained, and furthermore, it is also possible to be raised in one leap to the highest heaven, as Isaiah was.

Another aspect that seems to be ignored is the fact that in several places Pseudo-Denys tells the reader that he is writing *hymns*, not treatises, even though they are set out as prose (except for the introduction to the *Mystical Theology*, which is poetry). But I have yet to find an interpretation that takes this into account. Similarly, while Golitzin points to a Syriac cultural milieu, he is non-specific. Yet to read Ephrem's poem on metaphor in concert with the *Divine Names* or the *Celestial Hierarchy* (see especially CH144C–145B), or the *Mystical Theology* in concert with John of Apamea's (John the Solitary's) astonishing text on the progressive levels of silence,[83] suggests that the Syriac connection may be more direct

---

82. For example, Jaroslav Pelikan, quoting *Epistle 8*: "He who does not bestow illumination is thereby excluded from the priestly order and from the power reserved to the priesthood. For he is unilluminated. . . . This is no priest. He is an enemy, deceitful, self-deluded, a wolf in sheep's clothing ready to attack the people of God." From the introduction to Luibheid and Rorem, *Pseudo-Dionysius*, 18.

83. John the Solitary again: "How long shall I be in the world of the voice and not in the world of the word? For everything that is seen is voice and is spoken with the voice, but in the invisible world there is no voice, for not even voice can utter its mystery. How long shall I be voice and not silence, when shall I depart from the voice, no

and specific than simple association or resonance. Pseudo-Denys hates definition as much as Ephrem does, and he uses symbols in the same way as Ephrem. He is just as acute psychologically as John of Apamea in his understanding of the mind's work with silence. While he is often labelled "Neoplatonist," it should be remembered that he is writing from the point of view of psychology, of praxis; in some places he even seems to apologize for using language that may seem too Platonic. In certain phrases or concepts such as "gathered into one," or even the One, which are often interpreted by scholars as Neoplatonic, he could just as well have been alluding to the *Didache*, the Psalms, or the Gospels, all of which use the same language. Neoplatonic language is the *lingua franca* of his milieu, but he does not seem particularly comfortable with it, and as a Syrian, his mentality, whatever his education, appears to be soaked in Semitic culture.

The point here is not to begin a study of Pseudo-Denys, for which there is neither time nor space, but simply to suggest that we become so accustomed to hearing or reading about certain authors in received interpretations that even attempts to start again can be short-circuited if one is intimidated by the work that has gone before. Such work is not to be discounted, but it should also not become such a sacred cow that it cannot be challenged, especially when one is being told directly what is going on by the author, as in the case of Pseudo-Denys' remarks that he is writing hymns. It almost seems ridiculous to have to proffer a reminder to *read the text that is written*, but centuries and layers of interpretation can cloud our eyes, just as today's more linear and literal ways of reading make it necessary to remind us that in certain texts *all meanings are meant* as we saw earlier.

In this chapter we have looked at some of the tropes (and traps) that can enhance our reading of texts concerning the interior life. The goal once again is not to approach such texts as a game of "I-spy-with-my-little-eye," but rather to understand that many of these strategies can open in the text portals to silence by which we may enter if we are alert to them, and listen for the way words resonate in the physical-mental continuum of our bodies. This is particularly true of paradox, as noted in the previous volume, and we shall look at paradoxes in more depth in the New Testament chapter.

---

longer remaining in things which the voice proclaims? When shall I become word in an awareness of hidden things, when shall I be raised up to silence, to something which neither voice nor word can bring." Quoted in Brock, "John the Solitary, *On Prayer*," 87.

Before that, however, I want to look at some apophatic words and phrases in the Old Testament. We have seen in this chapter that there are apophatic images, and apophatic phrases, and that paradoxes act in an apophatic way, but these characteristics are also exhibited by individual words that in themselves are portals to silence, and it is to these that we now turn.

[There is a] relationship between the ascent of the mind through negations, addressed most directly in The Mystical Theology, and the "uplifting" or anagogical understanding of both biblical and liturgical symbols in the two hierarchical treatises. . . . The ancient and medieval view of scriptural and ritual symbols involved both subtle theories of the cognitive process and the conviction that this process was not just a matter of human will and skill but a spiritual journey through the symbols to God . . . .[84]

84. Rorem, *Biblical and Liturgical Symbols*, 9.

TWO

Old Testament Silence

I don't think of it [the Bible] as a "sacred" book, though sacred spaces can open when reading it. That is to say, the sacredness is contingent upon the reader's engagement and openness, her willingness to listen and be changed. It is a quality activated by consciousness and by a heart at risk, rather than something latent in the text.

—CHRISTIAN WIMAN[1]

Vladimir Lossky spoke of a "margin of silence" belonging to the words of Scripture, "which cannot be picked up by the ears of those outside." Only those who can discern this margin of silence are able to enter into the real meaning of the Scriptures. It is only in a spirit of prayer that we can become attuned to this silence.

—ANDREW LOUTH[2]

The innermost meanings, hidden behind the literal sense of the words on the page, were not only the most profound, but also only available to those with eyes to see.

—ORIGEN[3]

The desire of monks and mystics is not unlike that of artists: to perceive the extraordinary within the ordinary by changing not the world but the eyes that look. Within a summoned and hybrid aware-ness, the inner reaches out to transform the outer, and the outer

1. Christian Wiman, "Nimble Believing," in Kaminsky and Towler (eds.), *A God in the House,* 247–48.

2. Louth, *Dionysius,* 44.

3. Origen, quoted in McGilchrist, *The Master and His Emissary,* 152.

reaches back to transform the one who sees. . . . The prize of vision arrives unsought, as grace, while our more purposeful consciousness sleeps . . . .

—JANE HIRSHFIELD[4]

READING HAS BEEN CONTROVERSIAL from ancient times, but the reading and interpretation of texts that explore what is commonly regarded as "the sacred" particularly so. The objections are many: reading destroys the mind's ability to remember; texts are dangerous if they fall into the "wrong" hands; sacred texts may be interpreted in heterodox ways; universal literacy threatens the control exercised by the state. In this regard, few texts have been as controversial as the Bible, and for centuries—literacy issues aside—it was forbidden for ordinary people to read and interpret it.[5]

People have used the Bible to justify war and to argue for peace; to defend slavery and promote liberation. It has been said that anything can be proved from the Bible. Methods for reading and interpreting the Bible have abounded from its inception, from the plain "literal" sense to the anagogical interpretation alluded to by the quotation from Origen above.[6] Augustine regarded Bible reading as a spiritual quest:

> Augustine indicated that though Scripture can be read by all with "ease," it also "has a deeper meaning in which its great secrets are locked away." These secrets require that reading be conducted as a spiritual and contemplative activity. Consequently, for the Christian reader, reading constituted an act of interpretation for accessing meaning and truth. . . . Augustine believed that Christian reading "lifted the veil of mystery, and disclosed the spiritual meaning of texts which, taken literally, appeared to contain the most unlikely doctrines." . . . [T]he Augustinian approach to reading . . . has been described by one scholar "as seeking epiphanies between the lines."[7]

4. Hirshfield, *Ten Windows*, 12, 22.

5. For a recent study see Furedi, *Power of Reading, passim.*

6. The various senses in which Scripture can be read were first named by Origen. By the early Middle Ages these developed into four senses: literal, historical, moral, and anagogical. The anagogical sense concerns the way Scripture can lead the soul to God; it is the "spiritual," even eschatological way of interpretation.

7. Furedi, *Power of Reading*, 42.

Over time, this anagogical sense has fallen into disuse among scholars, especially those of the last two centuries, who discarded it for historical-critical methodologies, to the benefit of historical knowledge, cultural insight, and literary origins, but to the detriment of translations, which are now banal and flat, and do not reflect the contemplative depth of many biblical texts or the original languages in which they are written.

For the last two centuries there has been a growing tendency to read the Bible literally instead of literarily; that is to say, there has been a rise of so-called literal interpretations, which are applied detrimentally even to passages that are obviously poetic and symbolic. This is a literalism that is very different from the "plain sense" of the Late Antique and medieval worlds, or even that of the Reformation.

The flattening of texts by dumbing down or ignoring the metaphorical and anagogical level of texts is not confined to the Bible. There appears to be a widespread tendency to take away—deliberately or through ignorance—the need for deep reading or attentive listening, not to mention the joy of discovery. In an article in the *Guardian*, Tom Sutcliffe writes:

> Her [Emma Rice's] instance was taken from *Cymbeline*, the only Shakespeare play she has directed to date. She hadn't known, she explained, that the line "Golden lads and girls all must, / As chimney sweepers come to dust" contained a reference to the Warwickshire slang for dandelions. Replace "chimney sweepers" with "dandelions," she suggested, and nobody will be left out. Except, of course, all those who cherish the way the image trembles between the botanical and the human. Make that change and a living metaphor is flattened into a pressed flower. And the most poignant suggestion, that life coats the most gilded of us in the soot of experience, is gone completely. If you have to choose between partial understandings better, surely, to go with Shakespeare and let some discover later how much lies in the line. The discovery is a pleasure in itself.[8]

Here is an example of a flattened Bible translation: Isaiah 33:17 says, "Your eyes will see [Heb. behold] the king in his beauty; they will behold a land that stretches far away." The first Hebrew word translated "see" in the passage has nuances of what is seen by a seer; the second, translated "behold" what the seer interprets from his beholding. In this NRSV translation, the translator has chosen the weaker of the Hebrew words to translate with the word "behold," thus scrambling the sequence of sense

8. Sutcliffe, "In Defense of Shakespeare's Difficult Bits," *Guardian*, 6 January 2016.

so that the account of what is thought to have been seen has more weight than the pre-conceptual vision that bestows it; that is to say, the NRSV translation gives more weight to the interpretation than to the original perception.

From another point of view, it would be easy to pass over this verse as part of the prophetic context in which it appears, but the alert reader might recognize it not only as an eschatological prophecy, but also as an allusion to the spacious interior silence of the heart. In this light, the passage becomes a portal through which the reader may enter into the liminal, a passage to deep silence.[9]

It is the discovery of these portals into silence that this volume seeks to explore, as opposed to entertaining controversies over dating, redactions, and other textual problems that face the biblical scholar. In this sense, this book differs from others because it is far more about the eye of the reader's heart than the construction/context/redaction of the text itself. Having said that, it is impossible to address all of the possibilities by which these portals may be found—they differ for each reader—and in this chapter I will focus primarily on examples of how the model of the mind presented in Volume 1 can be uncovered in various passages, and on what I call apophatic words, which, like the apophatic images discussed in the previous chapter, open the mind, the eye of the heart, into the liminal, into beholding.

———◆———

The word *behold*—which will be explored at greater length in the last chapter of this volume—serves both functions. Its presence—and it is one of the most frequently occurring words in the ancient languages of the Bible, even though it is for the most part omitted in modern translation—signals a shift in perception; that is to say, the linear and interpreted opens to the direct perception of the deep mind for expansion, depth, and insight, a paradox of optics that grants simultaneously a sharper focus and a greater depth of field. In addition, *behold* functions as an apophatic word, bringing the mind to a halt, initiating a silence, an opening, and a receptivity that is pre-conceptual, without image or object, that initiates in the reader the radical relinquishment that opens a space for the dislocation and insight that are to come.

9. Zwingli seems to have understood the need for silence, even if he did not understand music as a portal to silence. See the discussion in MacCulloch, *Silence*, 132.

The very first occurrence of *behold* in the Bible is the very first word of direct speech that God makes to the human beings he has created in Genesis 1:29. This speech differs in character from the chthonic, silent words of creation and blessing (1:28) which have gone before.[10] It is followed by a second occurrence, the narrator's emphatic *behold* (1:31) that affirms the goodness of the creation. In the first occurrence, *behold* serves not only to create the awed silence in which God's direct speech may be heard, but also signals the shift to direct speech itself. The silence it creates is not only for the man and the woman to whom God is speaking but for all of creation and the reader as well. It is a silence outside of time that resonates the silent and creative Word throughout the cosmos.

By contrast, in the second creation story in chapter 2, the creation of the animals and even the creation of the garden itself follows *after* the creation of man, so that the first earthly relationships Adam has is with the animals he is to name (2:19–20)—but, again, this naming is not direct speech. The narrative simply tells us that God brought the animals to Adam to see what he would name them, after God muses to himself that it is not good for man to be alone (2:18). The first occurrence of direct speech in this account takes place when God forbids man to eat of the tree of the knowledge of good and evil, after the creation of the garden but before the creation of the animals. There are no occurrences of *behold* in chapter 2, which seems altogether more like a folktale when compared to the grandeur of 1:1 to 2:3, although this more informal and linear form does not mean that there is a lack of truth in the account.

In this second version of the creation story, there is nothing about the creation of the heavens and the earth; the story is altogether more piecemeal. There is no sequence of days of creation, rather there is a Day of creation—the sense of timelessness in the second account is broken by the direct speech of God's negative command to the man. It is as if in the first

10. Cf. Psalm 19: "Although there is no speech nor language, and their voice is not heard, yet is their sound gone out into all lands and their message to the ends of the earth" (composite translation). In regard to this psalm, Hirshfield writes, "silence washes back into the unheard voice and charges it further" (*Ten Windows*, 295).

Consider Rabbi Benjamin J. Segal's translation of Ps 65:1, "To you silence [also "waiting" *dumiyyah*] is praise, God, in Zion; a vow to You will be paid."

Hirshfield comments: "The quietist poem is not silence, yet its words might add to the portion of silence around them" (ibid., 273). And the same author: "'What is more important,' the Swiss novelist Max Frisch wrote, 'is what cannot be said, the white space between the words.' The Czech poet Miroslav Holub said in a *Paris Review* interview, 'In a broader sense, all poetry aims for the silence between and after the words. . . . Poetry should use a minimum of words for a maximum of conceived silence'" (ibid., 296).

account the sense of timelessness endures, while in the second account, time seems to begin with God's admonishment to the man. The direct speech in chapter 1 is positive; the direct speech in chapter 2 is negative. The first might be called a continuous beholding that engages God with the creation, while the second gives an entirely different sense: it is as if God is waiting to see what his creation is going to do: there is an almost cat-and-mouse sense, after that negative command is given. And, unsurprisingly, the first and only *behold* (3:22) in this second story expresses God's surprised outrage that the man and woman have transgressed and have eaten the fruit of the tree of the knowledge of good and evil.

In terms of the models of the mind, it is almost as if the first version of the story is the one the deep mind tells, and the second the version that the self-conscious mind tells. Or we might say that the chaos out of which God makes creation in the first story is an image of the self-conscious mind being worked on by the deep mind, while the creation that God beholds as good is a type of the optimal flow of the deep mind freely exchanging with the self-conscious mind.[11]

If, however, we read the two accounts as one story, which was common in the Late Antique and Middle Ages, we might say that until the moment the serpent initiated the first conversation, God and the humans beheld one another, but when the serpent distracted Adam and Eve from their beholding, this *distraction* constituted "the Fall" (a term that does not occur in the Bible). Indeed, as we saw in the previous volume, this was the understanding of many patristic and monastic writings: that the greatest sin is not pride, or disobedience, but rather distraction from beholding, that is to say, being distracted by self-consciousness and conversation.

For Adam and Eve, beholding had been their lodestar; after they became distracted from beholding, they lost their sense of direction and became anxious and afraid. We could read the rest of the story—their being driven from the garden, the curses—as a kind of hallucination arising from their anxiety and sense of disorientation. In reality, God's love has not abandoned them—indeed, God's "wrath" is the relentless love that pursues them—and manifests in a very practical way: God makes them clothes. But the consequences, both symbolic and practical, are that we, the children of Adam and Eve, must struggle through and with

11. We might even speculate that time-traveling verbs in Hebrew may reflect an implicit understanding of this structure of the mind, which, once again, anyone can realize by observation.

distraction until we find our way back to beholding. In reality, we have never left the garden and the beholding of God which indwell the center of the deep mind; but now access to it is not a given: instead, we have to make the journey to that realization through a repeated iconoclasm of the ideas and concepts generated by the self-conscious mind so that they may be deepened by the deep mind.

We might go so far as to say that the entire message of the Bible can be summarized in this one word: *behold*. All that God has ever asked of his creation is to *behold*: to behold God, to behold one another and the creation, to behold the goodness that is self-outpouring love. In Isaiah 65:1 God cries, "Behold me! Behold me!" poorly translated as "Here am I, here am I," which gives a completely different meaning and voice to the passage, which is emphatic.

> I was ready to be sought by those who did not ask for me;
> I was ready to be found by those who did not seek me.
> I said, "Here am I, here am I," [Heb: "Behold me, behold me"] to a
> nation that did not call on my name.
> I spread out my hands all the day to a rebellious people,
> who walk in a way that is not good,
> following their own devices . . . .
> Behold, it is written before me:
> "I will not keep silent, but I will repay,
> yea, I will repay into their bosom
> their iniquities and their fathers' iniquities together . . . .
> Behold, my servants shall eat,
> but you shall be hungry;
> behold, my servants shall drink,
> but you shall be thirsty;
> behold, my servants shall rejoice,
> but you shall be put to shame;
> behold my servants shall sing for gladness of heart,
> but you shall cry out for pain of heart,
> and shall wail for anguish of spirit . . . .
> So that he who blesses himself in the land
> shall bless himself by the God of truth,
> and he who takes an oath in the land
> shall swear by the God of truth;
> because the former troubles are forgotten
> and are hid from my eyes."
> (Isa 65: 1–2, 6–7, 13–14, 16)[12]

12. See Fretheim, *The Suffering of God*, 119.

This passage has strong echoes of the second creation story, and the suffering recounted in it is the suffering of consequence, of the refusal to behold. Although the prophet's words entail a conventional notion of divine vengeance ("I will repay"), in reality, as the author makes clear, God is always ready with open hands to receive even those who do not seek him. The passage is far more about the blessings of seeking to behold and ultimate reconciliation than it is about the consequences of not beholding.

Old Testament authors sometimes take the theme of God's seeking after those who do not seek him or who seem to oppose him to radical lengths. In Isaiah 45:1–7, the prophet goes so far as to put these words in God's mouth:

> Thus says the LORD to his anointed, to Cyrus
> whose right hand I have grasped,
> to subdue nations before him
> and ungird the loins of kings,
> to open doors before him
> that gates may not be closed:
> I will go before you
> and level the mountains,
> I will break in pieces the doors of bronze
> and cut asunder the bars of iron,
> I will give you the treasures of darkness
> and the hoards in secret places,
> that you may know that it is I, the LORD,
> the God of Israel, who call you by your name.
> For the sake of my servant Jacob,
> and Israel my chosen,
> I call you by your name,
> I surname you, though you do not know me.
> I am the LORD, and there is no other,
> besides me there is no God;
> I gird you, though you do not know me,
> that men may know, from the rising of the sun
> and from the west, that there is none besides me;
> I am the LORD, and there is no other.
> I form light and create darkness,
> I make weal and create woe,
> I am the LORD, who do all these things.

The meaning of "treasures of darkness" is not necessarily confined to gold and material booty. Even Cyrus may enter the deep places of the mind, the dazzling darkness, to know the Lord.

"Behold me" also occurs in 1 Samuel 3. Samuel's response to Eli and God is usually translated, "here am I," but again the Hebrew is "behold me." Isaiah himself (6:8) says in the context of the tremendous vision he is given: "Behold me." And the same *behold me* appears in the New Testament (Luke 1:38) when Mary says, "Behold, I am the handmaid of the Lord." It is reciprocal beholding that is the subject of the Bible, how God seeks beholding with us always; how humankind too often spurns beholding, and the inexorable and dire consequences that follow on when we do; the unimaginable blessings when we manage to return, behold, and be healed (Isa 6:10).[13] Here again are echoes of the creation story, and its eschatological outcome:

> For behold, I create new heavens and a new earth;
> And the former things shall not be remembered
> or, come into mind.
> But be glad and rejoice for ever
> in that which I create;
> for behold, I create Jerusalem a rejoicing,
> and her people a joy.
> I will rejoice in Jerusalem,
> and be glad in my people . . . .
> Before they call I will answer,
> while they are yet speaking, I will hear.
> The wolf and the lamb shall feed together,
> the lion shall eat straw like the ox;
> and dust shall be the serpent's food.
> They shall not hurt or destroy
> in all my holy mountain, says the LORD.
> (Isa 65:17–19, 25)

The first three chapters of Genesis underlie many of the allusions and prophecies in the Bible. Over and over again, from one generation to another, writers have offered varying interpretations of these stories. And this is as it should be, for the Bible offers many passages where *all meanings are meant,* even if at times the meanings seem paradoxical or even contrary. This does not mean that all interpretations are equal, far from it: discernment is required as to which interpretation is appropriate

13. Or, "turn and live" (Ezek 18:32). Variations of this phrase are scattered throughout the Bible.

in context—while not discounting the others—and discernment takes a lifetime to learn.

It is hard for us, living as we are in an increasingly linear and digitally defined culture that does not allow for paradox and ambiguity, to understand and to accept that especially with texts such as those in the Bible there is rarely, if ever, one unequivocal meaning; and that, contrary to what some modern biblical scholars would have us believe, there is every justification for interpretation that illuminates the personal and the interior, which has a long and honored history in Hebrew religions, Judaism and Christianity. This polysemous character is one of the signs of a great and enduring text, and reading a book such as the Bible is *for the ordinary reader* far more like the free association of psychoanalysis than the parsing of sentences. As Jane Hirshfield reminds us, "What we think of as 'art' . . . makes the encounter with the uncertain a thing to be sought. . . . To exchange certainty for praise of mystery and doubt is to step back from hubris and stand in the receptive, both vulnerable and exposed."[14]

Or, as the old joke tells us, where there are ten rabbis, there are twelve opinions. In the rabbinic way of interpretation, which follows strict rules, even the individual letters have significance.

> In the imagery of Islam, paradise is a walled garden; the Hebrew word from which our English "paradise" comes is *pardes,* whose ordinary meaning is orchard. Kabbalists map how an orchard becomes the dwelling place of the sacred by showing the hidden meaning that resides in each of its letters. "P" stands for *peshat,* the mind that sees the world literally; "r" for *remez,* the understanding of allusion and metonymy; "de" is for *derash,* metaphoric or symbolic interpretation; and "s" for *sod*—"secret." There is no paradise, no place of true completion, that does not include within its walls the unknown.[15]

Here is some rabbinic interpretation that illustrates the personal and the interior interpretation of Scripture. The author, Martin Krava, is quoting Emmanuel Levinas:

> R. Nachman said: If he [the Messiah] is among those living, it might be one like myself, as it is written: "And his chieftain shall be one of his own [lit. from him], and his ruler [*moshlo*] will come out of his innermost [places]" (Jer 30:21).

14. Hirshfield, *Ten Windows,* 123.
15. Hirshfield, *Ten Windows,* 115–16.

Jeremiah's text concerns an age in which sovereignty will return to Israel. The Messiah is . . . the absolute interiority of government. Is there a more radical interiority than the one in which the ego masters itself [*commande à lui-même*]? . . . The Messiah is the King who no longer commands from outside— this idea of Jeremiah's is brought by R. Nachman to its logical conclusion: The Messiah is myself [*Moi*]; to be myself is to be the Messiah.[16]

Krava goes on to remark: "Thus, this section of the Talmud proclaims the Messiah to be someone who literally touches—dare one say caresses?—from the depths of his or her interior spaces . . . ."[17]

⸺⸱⸺

Let us look at some more passages where the model of the mind might be found. These interpretations are personal portals to silence, and not to be taken as the only way or even a "legitimate" (according to some biblical scholars) way to interpret these particular texts, but rather a personal option that might be useful for one's interior life. At the same time, it is not surprising—as we shall see with the passages that use apophatic words—that among these texts are many of the most familiar passages of the Bible: readers/hearers may be caught by the silence in them even though unaware that it is the silence that holds them, the sense that there is "something more" going on in the text that cannot be grasped. Again, a note of caution: just because these passages and others *can* be interpreted this way does not mean they *ought* to be interpreted this way: the purpose of this volume is to show some ways that we might find portals into silence through the texts and through liturgy, not to address technical questions of textual criticism.

Genesis 22:1–19 tells the horrific story of Abraham's near-sacrifice of Isaac. This is another passage which, like Genesis 1–3, has received multiple interpretations. Some of them try to explain away the terror; some face it head-on. Many emphasize the trauma inflicted on Isaac no matter how positive the outcome, or outrage that Abraham would interpret God's words the way he does.

For our purposes, there are a number of things to note. Abraham says "Behold me!" three times: once to God, once to Isaac, and once to

16. Levinas, "Textes Messianiques," 119–20, translated by Seán Hand as "Messianic Texts," in *Difficult Freedom*, 88–89.

17. Krava, *Jewish Messianism*, 177–78.

the "angel of the LORD" who stays his hand. These expressions signal his willingness in obedience and anguish to open to the deep mind from which the voice of God emerges. Whether or not Abraham initially interprets that voice correctly is a question too complex to address here. But perhaps we should pay attention to the fact that he keeps repeating his openness to beholding so that his interpretation can be corrected. Perhaps this repeated openness in the face of the unthinkable is the key to understanding this horrific text.

Next, we might interpret Isaac as the construct of our selves, our self-image (as opposed to the unfolding truth of our selves) that we grasp and protect as if our lives depended on it—the only "child," as it were, of our human creation. In this view, the passage tests our willingness to let go this construct in order to taste of the reality of our own unfolding truth in God whose influence can emerge from deep mind only when we are able to set our self-image aside.[18]

This process of setting self-image aside can be very traumatic, especially in the beginning of praxis. There are also a lot of misinterpretations in the literature of the interior life that say that the self-image or the "false self" needs to be "destroyed," or "annihilated"—a mistaken dichotomy that has no foundation biblically or psychologically; there is no "true" or "false" self: we need *all* of our selves to grow into God. This dualism is entirely wrong, biblically, theologically, and psychologically. First, we do not have God's perspective and should not presume to judge what is "true" or "false" in our selves; second, it is the whole of us that needs transfiguring (the creation is intrinsically good, remember, and it is our perspective that is warped); and, thirdly, that transfiguring process often takes place through the most wounded, the most traumatized places in us.

But the point here is that we must be willing to go as far as the stage of the third "Behold me!" in the Abraham and Isaac story, when it feels as though the knife is at our own throat, as it were, so that we may be open to and given another option represented by the ram in the thicket: we may realize the unreality of the construct of self—that it is not in fact our truth but an expendable mask that we present to the world and even to God. Here the typology tends to break down, but this sort of interpretation is not meant to be allegorical. Rather, the message is that while we think we may have opened enough to live in beholding, there is always

---

18. It only *feels* as if it is set aside; rather it is our attention that shifts away from our closely guarded construct, leaving that construct open to be changed.

something we are holding back, and the prying open of our hands to offer our selves to be transfigured—our perspective slain and given back to us, clarified and expanded—is always going to be traumatic. We can never come away from an encounter with the divine without being profoundly changed, change that usually comes through our woundedness.

The stories of Jacob's vision of the ladder (Gen 28:10–32) and his wrestling with God (Gen 32:22–32) can be similarly interpreted; in both these stories the silence is implicit. The first appears quite simple: the dream-vision comes when he is asleep, when his self-consciousness is set aside; the word "behold" occurs three times in the telling. Jacob's wrestling with God could be understood as follows: he has sent ahead of him to appease Esau all that is precious to him, all those possessions and people by which he defines himself. As night falls and he is alone, he wrestles with what is variously translated as "a man," "an angel," or "God," though it is clear that this being is divine, perhaps the divinity within him. As Terence Fretheim puts it in a remarkable statement from a remarkable book, "There is no such thing for Israel as a nonincarnate God."[19] God's theophanies in human form anticipate the incarnation. Jacob is wounded when God touches his thigh, and this wound opens him to his divinization, and this divinization gives him a new name, "Israel," indicating a person who is both human and divine. It cannot be said often enough that it is through our wounds that we come to divinization.

———

The image of a capricious and vindictive Old Testament God has arisen from careless and selective reading and interpretation by those teachers who would intimidate their congregations for reasons of control, and people such as Richard Dawkins who seek to discredit religion entirely. This has led to a bias against reading the Old Testament, even in liturgy; some people go so far as to say the Old Testament is irrelevant and should be entirely set aside. But there is no New Testament without the Old Testament; we cannot understand the textual, literary, theological, and cultural environment of the New Testament without its predecessor.[20] The New Testament frequently alludes to or directly quotes the Old

---

19. Fretheim, *The Suffering of God*, 106.

20. When I refer to the "Old Testament" I include the books known as the Apocrypha.

Testament; it is impossible to catch these allusions without a thoroughgoing knowledge of the Old Testament.[21]

One of the main problems with the stereotypical portrait of a violent and vindictive God is God's supposed attitude toward to power: people seem to misunderstand what omnipotence means. It is not zapping power or controlling power; it is rather the ability to weave into Providence whatever decisions our free will makes, whether we regard them as good or bad. This means that instead of focusing power on control, God focuses on a responsive salvation, which requires a kenotic (self-emptying) listening and response. One of the oldest meanings in Hebrew for salvation is being freed from a trap. God releases us from the traps we make for our selves when our self-consciousness shuts itself off from the deep mind, and gives us hope. This self-emptying love is found not only in the New Testament, as in Philippians 2:5–11,

> Have this mind among yourselves,
> which is yours in Christ Jesus,
> who, though he was in the form of God
> did not count equality with God
> a thing to be grasped,
> but emptied himself, taking the form of a servant,
> being born in the likeness of men.
> And being found in human form
> he humbled himself and became
> obedient unto death, even death on a cross.
> Therefore, God has highly exalted him
> and bestowed on him the name
> that is above every name,
> that at the name of Jesus
> every knee should bow,
> in heaven and on earth
> and under the earth,
> and every tongue confess that Jesus Christ is Lord,
> to the glory of God the father. (RSV Common Bible)

but also in the Old Testament, for example the Servant Songs, which it mirrors:

> Surely he has borne our griefs
> and carried our sorrows;
> yet we esteemed him stricken,

---

21. See, for example, Fenton, *Finding the Way through Mark*, 43.

smitten by God, and afflicted.
But he was wounded for our transgressions,
he was bruised for our iniquities;
upon him was the chastisement that made us whole,
and with his stripes we are healed. (Isa 53:4–5, RSV Common Bible)

Or this, among the many, many passages that describe God's yearning
for his people to recognize and realize that God's love is immutable, and
willing to pay any price:

Hearken to me, O house of Jacob,
all the remnant of the house of Israel,
who have been borne by me from your birth,
carried from the womb;
even to your old age I am He
and to grey hairs I will carry you.
I have made and I will bear;
I will carry and I will save. (Isa 46:3–4)

God gives himself in the most intimate of ways, in spite of—or rather
because of—the apostasy of the people. Note again the allusion to the
Garden of Eden in the following:

Therefore, behold, I will allure her,
and bring her into the wilderness,
and speak tenderly to her . . .
and there she shall answer as in the days of her youth,
as at the time when she came out of the land of Egypt.
    "And in that day," says the LORD, "you will call me 'My
husband,' and no longer will you call me, 'My Baal . . .' I will remove the names of the Baals from her mouth, and they shall be
mentioned by name no more. And I will make you a covenant
that day with the beasts of the field, the birds of the air, and the
creeping things of the ground; and I will abolish the bow, the
sword, and war from the land; and I will make you lie down in
safety. And I will be troth you to me for ever; I will betroth you
to me in righteousness and in justice, in steadfast love, and in
mercy. I will betroth you to me in faithfulness; and you shall
know the LORD." (Hos 2:14-20)

The metaphors that are used for God in the Old Testament "are especially
important because Israel believed that 'The pattern on which man was

fashioned is to be sought outside the sphere of the created.'"[22] For example, the metaphor of maleness that is traditionally applied to God should not be dismissed outright as some feminist theologians and advocates of political correctness would have it. It is far more astonishing in our general cultural perception even today that a male rather than a female would have mercy and tenderness; that a male would bridge the ontological gap in self-emptying love; that a male would grieve. The male pronoun acts metaphorically, emphasizing the infinite extent of God's reach across the otherwise unbridgeable gap between the divine and human.

Yet another problem has arisen from the traditional idea that God is impassible. While the idea of the suffering of God was known to the early church, it is only in the latter half of the twentieth century through the present day that the subject of the suffering of God has come into the open in mainstream theology.[23]

> The idea that openness to suffering might be an index of the divine nature was developed in early Christianity, for example in the "hymn" in Phil. 2:5–11, especially if we interpret the line that says Christ did not see equality with God as *harpagmon* as meaning that he did not see it as expressed in "grasping-ness" ("did not regard equality with God as something to be exploited," NRSV): hence that *kenosis* is of the very nature of God himself. This risks the Christian heresy known as patri-passianism, the doctrine that the Father suffers, but one could retort that it is a heresy only because suffering was seen as a limitation on God's nature. If we believe in God's *Leidfreiheit* [freedom to suffer], we may say that God is known most fully in Christ because Christ shows just how far it is the nature of God to empty himself out on behalf of his creatures. Such an idea has also been expressed by a number of modern Christian theologians: alongside Paul Fiddes, one thinks of course of Moltmann, and (with Edmond Jacob) of Kazoh Kitamori. (This despite the long-established opposition to the idea that God could suffer in traditional Christianity.)[24]

22. Fretheim, *The Suffering of God*, 10, quoting von Rad, *Old Testament Theology*, vol. I:46.

23. See the excellent article by John Barton, "God, the World, and Wisdom." Barton cites precedents in Judaism for the suffering of God. There are medieval precedents for the understanding of God's grief. See for example, Ellen M. Ross, *The Grief of God*.

24. Barton, "God, the World and Wisdom," 22. He cites N. T. Wright, "*Harpagmos*," 321–52.

Barton quotes Jürgen Moltmann when describing the arguments against the existence of God marshalled by "protest atheists" such as Albert Camus, and suggests that these arguments are indeed powerful against God as sometimes conceived in Christianity, especially in its more philosophical strains:

> [A] God who cannot suffer is poorer than any man. For a God who is incapable of suffering is a being who cannot be involved. Suffering and injustice do not affect him. And because he is so completely insensitive, he cannot be affected or shaken by anything. He cannot weep, for he has no tears. But the one who cannot suffer cannot love either. So he is also a loveless being. Aristotle's God cannot love, he can only be loved by all nondivine beings by virtue of his perfection and beauty, and in this way draw them to him. The "unmoved Mover" is a "loveless Beloved." If he is the ground of the love (*eros*) of all things for him (*causa prima*), and at the same time his own cause (*causa sui*), he is the beloved who is in love with himself, a Narcissus in a metaphysical degree: *Deus incurvatus in se*. But a man can suffer because he can love, even as a Narcissus, and he always suffers only to the degree that he loves. If he kills all love in himself, he no longer suffers. He becomes apathetic. But in that case is he a God? Is he not rather a stone?[25]

To discuss all the theories of the suffering of God would require a book in itself. My own interpretation in *Pillars of Flame* is that God's impassibility is precisely the commitment to suffer with his people, a commitment to inviolable vulnerability.[26] As Frethiem puts it, "The grief of God is as current as the people's sin. . . . God's grief does not entail being emotionally overwhelmed or embittered by the barrage of rejection. Through it all, God's faithfulness and gracious purposes remain constant and undiminished."[27] Beholding in situations of Israel's sin or trouble signals God's grief, which makes him very different from the Stoic idea of God as immoveable in the sense of cold indifference; God is immoveable in his willingness to suffer with his people. Fretheim notes, quoting Abraham Joshua Heschel:

---

25. Barton, "God, the World, and Wisdom." The Moltmann quotation may be found in Moltmann, *The Crucified God*, 229.

26. Ross, *Pillars of Flame*, especially chapter 3.

27. Fretheim, *The Suffering of God*, 111.

"The speech that opens the book of Isaiah, and which sets the tone for all the utterances of the prophet, deals not with the anger of God but with the sorrow of God. The prophet pleads with us to understand the plight of a father whom his children have abandoned." It is important to note, in addition, that the focus is not on Israel's disobedience to an external legal code, but on the broken state of a re lationship between parent and child. Jesus' parable of the prodigal son cannot help but be recalled here.[28]

> Hear, O heavens, and give ear, O earth;
> for the LORD has spoken:
> "Sons I have reared and brought up,
> but they have rebelled against me.
> The ox knows its owner,
> and the ass its master's crib;
> but Israel does not know,
> my people does not understand . . . ;
> they have forsaken the LORD,
> they have despised the Holy One of Israel,
> they are utterly estranged" (Isa 1:2–3, 4b).

It is also important, echoing St. Paul (Phil 3:13), who in turn echoes the attitude of God in the Old Testament, to realize that we need to forget the past and look to the future, not only in our lives, but also in our interpretation. God is ready to forget the past and begin anew (as in the Isaiah 65:17 passage above, "For behold, I create new heavens and a new earth; /And the former things shall not be remembered or, come into mind."), and in response, we should be ready to forget what may have been our wrongful interpretation, for example, blaming God for consequences we have brought on ourselves. However sinful, violent, and dark the history of Israel in the Old Testament, the one constant through it all is the saving love of God. Authors may put dire warnings of retribution into the mouth of God, but almost invariably these are followed by words of encouragement and love (e.g., Hos 14:8). After accusing Israel of playing the harlot in 9:1, in 14:1–7, Hosea offers these words of comfort:

> I will heal their faithlessness;
> I will love them freely,
> for my anger and turned from them.
> I will be as the dew to Israel;
> he shall blossom as the lily,
> he shall strike root as the poplar;

28. Ibid., 114; Heschel, *The Prophets*, 79–80.

his shoots shall spread out;
his beauty shall be like the olive,
and his fragrance like Lebanon.
They shall return and dwell beneath my shadow,
they shall flourish as a garden;
they shall blossom as the vine,
their fragrance shall be like the wine of Lebanon.
O Ephraim, what have I to do with idols?
It is I who answer and look after you.
I am like an evergreen cypress,
from me comes your fruit. (RSV Common Bible)

Similarly, psalms of lament usually (but not always, e.g., Psalm 88:19 BCP 79) conclude with a statement of trust.[29] For example, Psalm 142:

I cry to the LORD with my voice;
to the LORD I make loud supplication.
I pour out my complaint before him
and tell him all my trouble.
When my spirit languishes within me, you know my path
in the way wherein I walk have they hidden a trap for me.
I look to my right hand and find no one who knows me;
I have no place to flee to, and no one cares for me.
I cry out to you, O LORD;
I say, "You are my refuge,
my portion in the land of the living."
Listen to my cry for help, for I have been brought very low;
save me from those who pursue me, for they are too strong for me.
Bring me out of prison, that I may give thanks to your Name;
when you have dealt bountifully with me,
the righteous will gather around me. (Psalm 143, BCP 79)

There are many direct references to silence in the Old Testament that can be used as portals. The desert is a prominent feature in the Old Testament, itself a place of profound silence. Then there is the silence of the holy of holies from which God speaks: "There I will meet with you, and from above the mercy seat, from between the two cherubim that are

29. Clifford, *Psalms 1–72*, 21. Clifford categorizes the following psalms as psalms of lament: 3–7; 9–10; 13–14; 17; 22; 25–26; 27:7–14; 28; 31; 35–36; 38–39; 41–43; 51; 53–54; 56–57; 59; 61; 63–64; 69–71; 86; 88; 102; 109; 120; 130; 139–43. Psalms of community lament: 44; 60; 74; 77; 79–80; 83; 85; 89; 90; 94; 123; 126.

upon the ark of the testimony, I will speak with you of all that I will give you in commandment for the people of Israel" (Exod 25:22). There is the "sheer silence" (NRSV) in which Elijah hears the voice of God (1 Kgs 19:11), the profound silence necessary to hearing God's voice.[30] Psalm 4:4 (BCP 79) directs the worshipper to "tremble, then, and do not sin; speak to your heart in silence upon your bed." Psalm 62:1, 6 sets an example for seeking the portals into silence: "For God alone my soul in silence waits; from him comes my salvation. . . . For God alone my soul in silence waits; truly, in him is my salvation" (BCP 79). "Be still [silent], and know that I am God" (Ps 46:11 RSV Common Bible). Wisdom 18:14 says, "When all things were in quiet silence, and the night was in the midst of her swift course, thine almighty world leaped down from thy royal throne" (liturgical translation). And Zephaniah commands, "Be silent before the Lord God!" (1:7 RSV Common Bible). But these references to silence are obvious. I want to turn now to the apophatic words with which the Old Testament is saturated.

Apophatic words operate in the same way as apophatic images: they stop the mind's chatter and give it a moment of *quies*, rest. Like apophatic images, apophatic words do not trigger images in the mind, but open on a vast inner space; they open the self-conscious mind to the deep mind.

The alert reader can use these words as portals to silence. When coming upon one of them, instead of continuing reading, the reader can indwell the moment of quiet created by the apophatic word, which in turn can indwell the reader and extend and broaden his or her inner vision. There are many of these words, and I will cite only a few:

---

30. There are places in the Alaska wilderness that are so silent that it almost seems as if one has become deaf.

anoint/oil of gladness, awe, beauty, behold, blameless, bless, bountiful, calm, contemplate, contentment, deep/depths, delight, exult/exalt, faith, fear, forever/everlasting, generous, glory, grace, greatness, healing, heart, hope, joy/gladness, laughter, light/name/countenance/ presence, majesty, laughter, love/ charity, longing, mercy, night watches, marvel/marvelous, meditate, overshadow/shadow, peace, ponder, protection/refuge, praise, promise, holy/holiness, wisdom, heart, solitude, interior, rapt, rest, refuge, safety, silence, seek, sorrow/weeping/tears, save/ salvation (narrow/wide), splendor, steadfast, stillness, thanksgiving, transfigure, transcend, trust, truth, unknowing, vision, wait, wonder, yearn

Equally there are apophatic words that create turmoil in the mind. Here are a few:

accuse, affliction, betray, blame, deep darkness, distress, faithless, foes/enemies, lost, lying/deceit, oppressors, panic, rage, rebuke, shame, tossed, trouble, turbulent

These lists only scratch the surface of apophatic words; each person may find more or different words that give either *quies* or chaos.

These words are scattered throughout the Bible, but cluster in the Psalms, poems that reflect every human emotion from praise to terror. Of the word *silence* in the Old Testament, a word that creates in the reader a moment of what it names, Alexander Ryrie notes:

> There are several Hebrew words which have to do with silence or quietness. . . . These words all carry the sense not only of silence but of waiting in silence or quiet expectation. . . . But there is also a silence which has to do with the relation of men and women to God. If people are to be in touch with God there needs to be a silencing or a quieting.
>
> It was true in relation to the temple worship, particularly in the rebuilt temple after the exile. . . . The appropriate response to the mystery of the presence of God was silence.[31]

We noted in Volume 1 of this book that the movement of the mind toward silence is a continuum in which the self-conscious mind gradually fades from awareness (awareness itself does not fade). Before we reach beholding, however, we must pass through the guardians, the cherubim with the flaming sword that protect the silence of beholding

31. Ryrie, *Silent Waiting*, 21–22. See von Rad, *Old Testament Theology*, vol. I, 242.

(Gen 3:24). The Psalms name and focus those emotions and thoughts that keep us outside the Eden of beholding in silence: our hopes, our fears, our joy and sorrow, our suffering, our regrets, our desire for vindication and salvation. These are the emotions that swirl around in our self-consciousness that can be stilled only by naming: as Adam, beholding, named the animals at their creation, so too we, struggling to behold, must name the obsessive thoughts that bar the way to our beholding in the depths of our hearts, our interior holy of holies, where we encounter other cherubim, those that overshadow the mercy seat where we behold the presence/face of God.[32]

As we become more familiar with the Bible, especially the Psalms, we build up an interior concordance that not only helps us recognize themes and allusions but also can serve as a signal to our selves as to the true nature of our interior life. There the Psalms turn slowly as it were, an interior prayer-wheel that sends our prayers floating on the wind of silence. These phrases arise from the deep mind to appear in our self-conscious mind as comfort, as warning, as praise. For example, we might get out of bed in the morning feeling out of sorts, but then realize that the phrase "I will bless the LORD at all times" (Ps 34:1 BCP 79) is turning in the backs of our minds, reminding us that our superficial feelings are just a lot of static, and that somewhere in the heart the psalm of praise and trust is turning, with such lovely phrases as "Look on him and be radiant, /and let not your faces be ashamed" (v. 5). Or "Taste and see that the LORD is good; /happy are they who trust in him" (v. 8). Or: "For in you is the well of life, /and in your light we see light." In sorrow, these words might arise: "Weeping may spend the night, but joy comes in the morning" (Ps 30:6 BCP 79). In a time of stress, being subject to too many demands, we might hear: "One thing have I asked of the LORD, one thing I seek; /that I may dwell in the house of the LORD all the days of my life; /To behold the beauty of the LORD /and to seek him in his temple." Or: "Out of Zion, perfect in its beauty, /God reveals himself in glory." Or: "Send out your light and your truth, that they may lead me, /and bring me to your holy hill and to your dwelling."

Or, we might be attracted to a new acquaintance in a positive way, only to have a psalm phrase emerge that contradicts our perception and warns us against capitulating to a superficial impression such as 35:9 (BCP 79): "Do not let my treacherous foes rejoice over me, do not let

---

32. Ross, *Pillars of Flame*, 127.

those who hate me without a cause wink at each other." Or: "But it was you, a man after my own heart [who betrayed me], /my companion, my own familiar friend. /We took sweet counsel together, /and walked with the throng in the house of God" (Ps 55:14–15 BCP 79). Or: "His speech is softer than butter, /but war is in his heart. /His words are smoother than oil, /but they are drawn swords" (Ps 55:22 BCP 79). Or in a time of desolation: "We walk about like a shadow, and in vain we are in turmoil; /we heap up riches and cannot tell who will gather them" (Ps 39:7 BCP 79). Our silent cry might express itself in the words of Psalm 55:7–9 (BCP 79): "Oh that I had wings like a dove! /I would fly away and be at rest. /I would flee to a far-off place /and make my lodging in the wilderness. /I would hasten to escape /from the stormy wind and tempest."

Psalm phrases rising from the heart can remind us in the ordinariness of our daily lives that no matter how fraught we may feel, we are still rooted, still living our lives in the love of God, that somewhere in our depths the Presence is always with us. The apophatic words of the Bible, but particularly of the Psalms, help to ground us in this continual beholding of the heart. We are reminded that in beholding our faces are radiant, reflecting God's radiance; we are comforted by God's goodness; dazzled by his glory; strengthened in his steadfastness; healed by grace through the gift of tears; grateful for mercy and salvation; vigilant in the night watches; overflowing with praise for God's mercy—the list goes on and on.

———

Finally, there is one more source of portals into silence I want to mention— though doubtless there are others—and that is *resonance*. Throughout the Bible there are images that have resonances that link with the resonances of similar images across both Old and New Testaments, creating a kind of echo chamber of charged silence.

The first example is that of empty space. The empty spaces of the Bible are potent, and there is an association among them as matrices of profound change. For example, the mercy seat between the cherubim (Exod 25:10 ff.), the cave of Elijah (1 Kgs 19:9), the womb of Mary (Luke 1:26 ff.), and the empty tomb (Luke 24:2 ff.). (Though not scriptural, we might include the Cave of the Nativity in our associations.) Each of these empty spaces are places of encounter and profound change. Each of these places is a source of new life or commission. In each of these places the voice of God or angel messengers are heard.

The mercy seat, where God speaks to Moses, is sheltered by cherubim. In front of Elijah's cave Elijah is told to anoint and crown two kings and to commission his successor, Elisha. Gabriel comes to announce to Mary that she will conceive Jesus by the Holy Spirit—we might note here that her conceiving is in the beholding; the rest of the sentence is for those who do not behold. There are angels ("two men") at the empty tomb (perhaps wearing the masks of tragedy and comedy) who announce the resurrection. Doubtless there are other examples of empty spaces not mentioned here.

Deserts, wildernesses, and mountains also feature in both Testaments: they too are places of change and beholding, particularly change of perspective. Hagar flees from an abusive Sarai into the wilderness (Gen 16:6b–14), but the voice of God persuades her to return. Exodus 3 tells the story of the burning bush, and when God calls to Moses from the flames on Mount Horeb (Mount Sinai), Moses replies, "Behold me" (Exod 3:4). The entire course of his life is changed by the command to lead his people out of Egypt. 1 Kings 18:20 ff. tells the story of Elijah's defeat of the prophets of Baal on Mount Carmel. He then moves on to Mount Horeb, where his encounter with the voice of God takes place at the mouth of the cave. Jesus is tempted in the desert (Matt 4 *passim*; Mark 1:12; Luke 4:1–13) to abuse the power he has been given, but instead he accepts his role and takes up his ministry. We could interpret this story as the occasion on which he rejects the deceptions of the self-conscious mind cut off from the deep mind, and chooses to continue in unbroken beholding. Again, this passage alludes to the events that took place in the Garden of Eden: though Adam and Eve failed their test, Jesus wins through. Mount Zion features throughout the Bible. It is the site of Jerusalem, and is the scene of many critical events.

John Fenton in his book on Mark suggests another theme, that of bread, which resonates through the Bible:

> [The feeding of the five thousand] is the only miracle that is recorded in all four gospels in almost identical words. There is, for example, the well-known Old Testament tradition concerning Moses and the manna in the wilderness; the story of Elisha feeding a hundred men with twenty barley loaves (they ate and had some left over); the expectation that the manna, the bread from heaven, would be eaten again in the age to come; the idea of eating bread as an image of salvation, participation in the feast of the age to come (Give us today the bread of tomorrow); and

the symbolism of the Eucharist. All or any of these may be there in the story of the feeding, waiting for the alert reader to pick them up . . . .[33]

The last conflation of associations I will mention (there are others) is that of radiance: the radiance of the face of Moses; the radiance of Elijah's chariot; the radiance of various angels that appear in both Testaments, the radiance of the human face in Psalm 34:5, the radiance of Transfiguration, the radiance both implicit and explicit in terms such as *glory, shining, face* [of God]. And *glory* is the subject of our next chapter.

---

33. Fenton, *Finding the Way through Mark*, 36–37.

THREE

New Testament Silence

*I think that in Heaven my mission will be to draw souls by helping
them to go out of themselves in order to cling to God by a wholly simple
and loving movement, and to keep them in this great silence within
which will allow God to communicate Himself to them and to transform them into Himself . . . "to the praise of his glory" (Eph 1:12,14).*

—ELIZABETH OF THE TRINITY (1880–1906) (EMPHASIS MINE)

God became human so that humans might become God.

—ATHANASIUS

Learn to be silent.

—1 THESS 4:11 (MY TRANSLATION).

BECOMING A PERSON, that is, realizing our shared nature with God (2 Pet
1:4), is accomplished by moving kenotically "from glory to glory" (2 Cor
3:18); and to the degree that we become a person through *kenosis* our
density makes a positive difference in the web of life analogous to the
image of the gravity of galaxies bending space-time. That is to say, our
personhood, our meaning, and our truth by grace come to mirror the
last verse of the prologue of the Gospel of John: "And the Word became
flesh and dwelt among us, full of grace and truth; we have beheld his
glory, glory as of the only Son from the Father" (John 1:14). This is rather
ploddingly translated in the NRSV as ". . . seen his glory" when the whole
point of the passage is that we *beheld*[1] his glory, that somehow there is a

---

1. It is shocking that the word *behold*, which occurs 234 times in the KJV, does not
occur at all in the NRSV translation of the New Testament and only twenty-seven times
in the NRSV Old Testament, whereas the Hebrew and Greek equivalents are found
throughout the Bible more than a thousand times. It is just as shocking that while there

divine exchange, a radical shift in perception and reality, which is emphasized throughout John's Gospel and the Johannine Epistles which precede it in historical time: "But to all who received him, who believed in his name, he gave power to become the children of God; who were born, not of blood nor of the will of the flesh nor of the will of man, but of God" (John 1:12–13).

Both Paul and John emphasize that we become temples of the Holy Spirit. Here is Paul:

> Do you not know that you are God's temple and that God's Spirit dwells in you? (1 Cor 3:16)

> Do you not know that your body is a temple of the Holy Spirit within you, which you have from God? You are not your own; 20 you were bought with a price. So glorify God in your body. (1 Cor 6:19–20)

> [Christ Jesus,] in whom the whole structure is joined together and grows into a holy temple in the Lord. (Eph 2:21)

> . . . but when a man turns to the Lord the veil is removed. Now the Lord is the Spirit, and where the Spirit of the Lord is, there is freedom. And we all, with unveiled face, beholding the glory of the Lord, are being changed into his likeness from one degree of glory to another; for this comes from the Lord who is the Spirit. (2 Cor 3:16–18)

In John 2:21 we read, "But he [Jesus] spoke of the temple of his body." Christ has "tabernacled" with us; that is to say, Christ has opened the way for his glory to descend into the tabernacle of our bodies (cf. Exod 40:34, "Then the cloud covered the tent of meeting;" John 1:14 lit. "the Word *tabernacled* among us"); 1 Cor 15:43 "[the body] is sown in dishonor, it is raised in glory."

---

are 136 occurrences of *glory* in the NRSV translation of the New Testament, there are 163 in the KJV, which is a word-for-word translation. There are many other theological distortions in this unfortunate modern translation. For example, it is also shocking that in the NRSV's translation of the Gospel of John, the word "faith" does not occur; the translator has failed to recognize the difference between faith and belief in modern English and has used "believe" in all eighty-five instances, translating the Greek *pistis*. While the Greek *pistis* does not distinguish between faith and belief, English *does* make this distinction and it is important theologically, as shown particularly in the Letter to the Hebrews: we have faith in what is unseen, unknowable, beyond concept, while we believe *in* a propositional statement. Faith is kenotic and open; belief claims.

The great high priestly prayer emphasizes the theme of unity in glory:

> ... that all may be one; even as thou, Father, art in me, and I in thee, that they also may be in us, so that the world may believe that thou hast sent me. The glory which thou hast given me I have given to them, that they may be one even as we are one, I in them and thou in me, so that they may become perfectly one ... (John 17:21–23)

The source and end of unity is divine glory, and in between, we participate in it in the temple/tabernacle of our bodies through the Spirit in our *kenosis* (e.g., 1 Pet 4:14; 5:4: "If you are reproached for the name of Christ, you are blessed because the Spirit of glory rests upon you"; "And when the chief Shepherd is manifested you will obtain the unfading crown of glory"). There is a huge paradox here: our weight, our density, our glory comes not through accumulation but through divestment, self-emptying. Divine glory is the opposite of human glory.

The descent of glory is a function of our beholding, our *kenosis* and, by implication, our knowledge of life in God. God's nature is self-outpouring (kenotic); this *is* his glory, his presence. To the degree that we mirror that self-outpouring in our kenotic beholding as the wellspring of our living, we realize our shared nature with the divine and we receive Christ's glory.[2] By contrast, the institution preoccupies us with all the medieval and Reformation hangovers that concentrate almost exclusively on sin and particularly the agony of the cross. Because of this, the theme of glory has been lost to the ordinary life of the church.[3] That is to say, we should understand "in the cross of Christ I glory" as "through the *kenosis* of Christ [manifested in my life] I share his glory."

The cross is symbolic of the action. It is not the object itself, but the disposition of the person of Jesus that leads to the cross that should be emphasized. This is the central paradox of the New Testament: *kenosis* is *glory*: "If you are reproached for the name of Christ, you are blessed, because the Spirit of glory and of God rests upon you" (1 Pet 4:14 cf. Matt 5:10–11). *Kenosis* is the veil that, as Isaac of Nineveh notes, "hid

---

2. It is perhaps significant that the word *know* occurs most often in the Gospel of John and the First Letter of John.

3. It is not cynicism but fact to note that the institution prefers to emphasize guilt because it makes people easier to control. This has been true in the West especially since Columbanus (d. 615) brought his sin-accounting system to mainland Europe as we saw in Volume 1.

the splendor of his majesty and concealed his glory with humility, lest creation be utterly consumed by the contemplation of him."[4] So it is with us: our *kenosis*, our self-forgetfulness, our beholding is hidden from our selves, from our self-consciousness, lest we be overcome by the manifestation of glory.

We should be clear that *kenosis* does not *lead* to glory, it *is* glory. The paradox is not comprehendible and moves us in awe and silence. Because words can only be linear and sequential, the hymn in Philippians 2:5–11 seems to suggest that *kenosis* leads to glory. But the *dio*, the *therefore*, at the bottom of the chiasmus is not QED. It is rather as if there is a cosmic intake of breath as the glory is revealed in the second half of the passage. We live in hope as Jesus lived in hope that this is the case; he had no guarantees that his self-outpouring would be his exaltation.

To repeat, language can only be sequential, but we must understand that *kenosis* and glory are two sides to the same coin. As we learn to live more and more kenotically, we proceed "from glory to glory" (2 Cor 3:18), that is, our density, the weight of our unfolding truth, increases and, as it were, creates a subtle atmosphere that affects those around us. *Kenosis* frees us from unlikeness and opens us to the divine exchange. The kabbalistic tradition suggests that there are only thirty-six holy people (*zaddikim*) in the world at any one time that keep it from being destroyed. In Christ we can hope that there are infinitely more such people; we might think of them as the weights, the densities, the anchors, in the membrane of existence, that keep the universe in motion and prevent it from dissolving into nothingness.

We might image the process as follows:

mind/heart → kenosis (humility/glory [implicit]) → transfiguration
→ tent/temple/heart → theosis/glory/humility [explicit]

But again, this image is misleading because it is sequential; degrees of deification happen all at once.

As audacious as the foregoing may sound, it is nonetheless entirely based in the New Testament, and as we have seen, its roots are in the silences of the Old Testament and Apocrypha (e.g., Wis 3:1–9: "But the souls of the righteous are in the hand of God . . .") with which it forms a chiasmus in terms of creation and beholding. Underneath all the moralizing and polemic in the New Testament, there is a message of divinization, *theosis*; that is to say, in the way appropriate to humans we may

---

4. Quoted in Alfeyev, *Isaac the Syrian*, 112.

once again through grace, by our *kenosis*, our self-forgetfulness in our lived beholding, realize our glory, our shared nature with God that was obscured in Eden, and all this entails. Furthermore, as we shall see, this theme, along with others, links the writings of Paul and the Gospels, even though in the West, at least, this understanding of *theosis*, or divinization has been buried under centuries of breast-beating and pious misinterpretation of what it means to be a child of God and an heir of Christ.

> There is no fear in love, but perfect love casts out fear. For fear has to do with punishment, and he who fears is not perfected in love. We love, because he first loved us. (1 John 4:18–20 RSV Common Bible)

It is not only the book of Revelation that is apocalyptic; the entire New Testament is an unveiling, a revelation that lifts the veil of *kenosis* a little to show us the Spirit of glory at work, just enough to encourage us in our *kenosis*, our beholding, but not so much that we are overcome. The word *glory*, when speaking of divine glory revealed, is itself a kind of veil; it is what I have earlier called an apophatic word; it is not a concept that we can grasp; quite the reverse. It breaks down any conceptualizations we might attempt, and defies any imaging to capture it. Apophatic words are kenotic words. They dazzle us, drawing us out from our ideas, particularly our ideas of our selves—the construct of self—into silence, in which our unfolding truth and divinity is revealed. *Glory* is *kenosis*, just as *kenosis* is *glory*. *Kenosis* reveals God's glory in us, most especially as we make room for it through the work of silence, which is itself *kenosis*. *Kenosis* is "the means of grace and the hope of glory," as the *Book of Common Prayer* puts it, echoing the Gospels (e.g., John 11:4, "This illness is not unto death; it is for the glory of God so that the Son of God may be glorified by means of it"; and 40: "Did I not tell you that if you would believe you would see the glory of God?"). While the whole of Jesus's life is kenotic, *kenosis*, and therefore glory, is particularly manifest in the healings. (E.g., Mark 5:30, "And Jesus, perceiving in himself that power had gone forth from him, immediately turned about in the crowd, and said, 'Who touched my garments?'" Luke 8:46, "And Jesus said, 'Who was it that touched me?'... But Jesus said, 'Someone touched me; for I perceive that power has gone forth from me.'")

The epigraph at the start of this chapter from Elizabeth of the Trinity, O.C.D. (d. 9 November 1906), shows her understanding of *kenosis* as glory. "To the praise of his glory" (the phrase occurs twice in two nearly adjacent verses Eph 1:12,14) is the focus of her life implicitly, and, towards the end of her life, explicitly, her constant refrain. Although comparisons are odious, in a way, her vision is more complete and mature than that of her contemporary Thérèse of Lisieux (d. 30 September 1897). Thérèse was focused on spiritual poverty, littleness, coming to God with empty hands (*kenosis*), but Elizabeth understood that these empty hands bear glory, and that this glory reveals the depths of our unfolding truth of *theosis*.

Even though the word *glory* (in the NRSV) occurs in the Epistles most often in Romans (ch. 15), Second Corinthians (ch. 14), and First Peter (ch. 10), the first three chapters of the Letter to the Ephesians might be called "the epistle of glory" because the words *glory* and *glorious* and reciprocal kenosis are central to its message, whether referring to our being raised with Christ (2:4–6, "But God . . . even when we were dead through our trespasses made us alive together with Christ . . . and raised us up with him, and made us sit in the heavenly places in Christ Jesus"), Paul's own suffering (3:11–12, "This was according to the eternal purpose which he has realized in Christ Jesus our Lord, in whom we have boldness and confidence of access through our faith in him"), or a doxology on the power of God working through our *kenosis* (3:20–21, "Now to him who by the power of work within us is able to do far more abundantly than all that we ask or think, to him be glory in the church and in Christ Jesus to all generations, for ever and ever. Amen" [doxologies have an apophatic effect on the reader/listener—see below]), even extending implicitly to the contentious passages in chapter 5 about wives and husbands. When read in terms of *kenosis*, especially following the opening admonition of *mutual* submission (5:21: "Be subject to one another out of reverence for Christ"), the apparent hierarchy of husband over wife is neutralized, for the command of *kenosis*, if anything, bears even greater weight on the man than the woman (e.g., 5:25: "Husbands, love your wives, as Christ loved the church and gave himself up for her"). In other words, the husband's attitude should be kenotic to the end.

The Epistles emphasize the roles of self-conscious mind and deep mind and their optimal relationship through a series of physical metaphors, e.g., Romans 6:5–8:

> For if we have been united with him in a death like his, we shall certainly be united with him in a resurrection like his. We know that our old self was crucified with him so that the sinful body might be destroyed, and we might no longer be enslaved to sin.

> For he who has died is freed from sin. But if we have died with
> Christ, we believe that we shall also live with him.

Here is another theme that unites the Epistles and Gospels: the con-
trasting in Paul's writings of "flesh" and "spirit," "flesh" meaning the un-
controlled lusts and passions that rule the self-conscious mind (e.g., Rom
13:14, "But put on the Lord Jesus Christ, and make no provision for the
flesh, to gratify its desires"), and "spirit" meaning the kenotic movement
towards deep mind. This is reflected in the Gospel of John, for example,
in the dichotomy between "the world" by which, among other things, he
means the corruption of the closed religious system (*kosmos* can mean
system) and the kenotic openness that leads to knowledge and unity with
Christ in glory (John 17:21–23 quoted above).

This theme is illustrated again in the famous passage in Romans 7
where Paul complains about doing what he doesn't want to do and not
doing what he does (7:21–25):

> So I find it to be a law that when I want to do right, evil lies close
> at hand. For I delight in the law of God, in my inmost self, but I
> see in my members another law at war with the law of my mind
> and making me captive to the law of sin, which dwells in my
> members. Wretched man that I am! Who will deliver me from
> this body of death? Thanks be to God through Jesus Christ our
> Lord! So then, I of myself serve the law of God with my mind,
> but with my flesh I serve the law of sin.

He delights in the law in his inmost self (his deep mind), but his passions and desires under the sway of his self-conscious mind—"the body
of death"—lead him to sin. This results in an inner conflict: his undisci-
plined desires cause him to serve the law of sin, but he knows that in his
deep mind, his unfolding truth serves the law of God through the grace
of Christ. *Theosis* doesn't happen all at once; it is a struggle that occupies
us until our last breath, yet one that contains hope. As Paul notes in the
following chapter: "For the law of the Spirit of life in Christ Jesus has set
me free from the law of sin and death."

Later in chapter 8, he speaks more specifically of the mind:

> For those who live according to the flesh set their minds on the
> things of the flesh, but those who live according to the Spirit set
> their minds on the things of the Spirit. To set the mind on the
> flesh is death, but to set the mind on the Spirit is life and peace.
> For the mind that is set on the flesh is hostile to God; it does not

submit to God's law, indeed it cannot; and those who are in the flesh cannot please God. . . .

But you are not in the flesh, you are in the Spirit, if in fact the Spirit of God dwells in you. . . . But if Christ is in you, although your bodies are dead because of sin, your spirits are alive because of righteousness. . . . [H]e who raised Christ Jesus from the dead will give life to your mortal bodies also through his Spirit which dwells in you. (Rom 8:5–8, 9–11b)

[handwritten margin note: flesh = images words concepts]

In these passages, Paul makes clear the seriousness of the choices we make with our minds, whether we live under the sway of the self-conscious mind, whose thoughts are derivative, artefact, and dead, and whose desires are inchoate, or whether we open our minds to receive the light and peace that the Spirit will give us. This is not a choice that is made once for all: it is a progressive kenotic movement ("from glory to glory") away from the self-conscious mind towards the predominance of the deep mind, inspired by love, responding to Love.

This movement eventuates in an interior stability that cannot be shaken (see also, e.g., Rom 15:4–6):

Who shall separate us from the love of Christ? Shall tribulation, or distress, or persecution, or famine, or nakedness, or peril, or sword? . . . No, in all these things we are more than conquerors through him who loved us. For I am sure that neither death, nor life, nor angels, nor principalities, nor things present, nor things to come, nor powers, nor height, nor depth, nor anything else in all creation, will be able to separate us from the love of God in Christ Jesus our Lord. (Rom 8:35, 37–39)

This closing doxology of chapter 8 acts apophatically on the reader's mind, as do doxologies in general in the New Testament. It is impossible to hold all the grand images at once in the conceptual mind, and in any event, much of what is mentioned is non-conceptual, mere gestures, jumping-off places into contemplation. Doxologies give us an apophatic glimpse of glory, an ineffable knowledge in our bodies ("gut knowledge"); they plunge us into the unfathomable reaches of the deep mind where we may rest in silence.

In Rom 9:23–24 Paul continues this theme of glory:

What if God . . . in order to make known the riches of his glory for the vessels of mercy, which he has prepared beforehand for glory, even us whom he has called, not from the Jews only but also from the Gentiles?

He clearly means the answer to be affirmative, as in 10:12–13:

> For there is no distinction between Jew and Greek; the same
> Lord is Lord of all and bestows his riches upon all who call upon
> him. For, "every one who calls upon the name of the Lord will
> be saved."

The kenotic way to glory through the re-focusing of the mind is summed
up in 12:1–2:

> I appeal to you therefore, brethren, by the mercies of God, to
> present your bodies as a living sacrifice, holy and acceptable to
> God, which is your spiritual worship. Do not be conformed to
> this world but be transformed by the renewal of your mind, that
> you may prove what is the will of God, what is good and accept-
> able and perfect.

Note that the body is essential to spiritual worship; the sacrifice of
kenosis may seem to be made by the mind alone, but this is not "minds
cut off from bodies;" we must never forget that in the world of Paul and
Jesus the word "mind" means "heart." It is the *whole person* that is kenotic, and it is the *whole person* that is glorified. Such a person lives in love,
and love is the fulfilling of the law (Rom 13:8, 10: "Owe no one anything,
except to love one another; for he who loves his neighbor has fulfilled the
law. . . . Love does no wrong to a neighbor; therefore love is the fulfilling
of the law").

> None of us lives to himself, and none of us dies to himself. If
> we live, we live to the Lord, and if we die, we die to the Lord; so
> then, whether we live or whether we die we are the Lord's. For to
> this end Christ died and lived again, that he might be Lord both
> of the dead and of the living. (Rom 14:7–9)

This knowledge enables us to live in hope:

> . . . he who rises to rule the Gentiles; in him shall the Gentiles
> hope. May the God of hope fill you with all joy and peace in be-
> lieving, so that by the power of the Holy Spirit you may abound
> in hope. (Rom 15:12–13)

Second Corinthians explores *theosis* in terms of the effects of divinization
in ordinary life. For example:

> Blessed be the God and Father of our Lord Jesus Christ, the
> Father of mercies and God of all comfort, who comforts us in
> all our affliction so that we may be able to comfort those who
> are in any affliction, with the comfort by which we ourselves
> are comforted by God. For as we share abundantly in Christ's
> sufferings, so through Christ we share abundantly in comfort
> too. If we are afflicted, it is for your comfort and salvation; and if
> we are comforted, it is for your comfort, which you experience
> when you patiently endure the same sufferings that we suffer.
> Our hope for you is unshaken; for we know that as you share in
> our sufferings, you will also share in our comfort. (2 Cor 1:3–7)

Second Corinthians 2:14 speaks of the fragrance, or aroma, of the knowledge of God that is spread through the disciples as they realize their
shared nature with God:

> But thanks be to God, who in Christ always leads us in triumph,
> and through us spreads the fragrance of the knowledge of him
> everywhere. For we are the aroma of Christ to God among those
> who are being saved and among those who are perishing, to one
> a fragrance from death to death, to the other a fragrance from
> life to life. . . . [I]n the sight of God, we speak in Christ.

Or again in 3:2–3, using the metaphor of writing:

> You yourselves are our letter of recommendation, written on
> your hearts, to be known and read by all men; and you show
> that you are a letter from Christ delivered by us, written not with
> ink but with the Spirit of the living God, not on tablets of stone
> but on tablets of human hearts.

Later in chapter 3, Paul makes one of his tortuous comparisons
between the glory in the face of Moses and the unveiled glory of those
who are proceeding "from glory to glory." This is the context of the "one
degree of glory to another" passage quoted above; the NRSV translates it
as follows:

> Now if the ministry of death, chiseled in letters on stone tablets,
> came in glory so that the people of Israel could not gaze at Mo-
> ses' face because of the glory of his face, a glory now set aside,
> how much more will the ministry of the Spirit come in glory?
> For if there was glory in the ministry of condemnation, much
> more does the ministry of justification abound in glory! Indeed,
> what once had glory has lost its glory because of the greater

glory; for if what was set aside came through glory, much more
has the permanent come in glory!

Since, then, we have such a hope, we act with great boldness,
not like Moses, who put a veil over his face to keep the people
of Israel from gazing at the end of the glory that was being set
aside. But their minds were hardened. Indeed, to this very day,
when they hear the reading of the old covenant, that same veil is
still there, since only in Christ is it set aside. Indeed, to this very
day whenever Moses is read, a veil lies over their minds; but
when one turns to the Lord, the veil is removed. Now the Lord
is the Spirit, and where the Spirit of the Lord is, there is freedom.
And all of us, with unveiled faces, seeing the glory of the Lord
as though reflected in a mirror, are being transformed into the
same image from one degree of glory to another; for this comes
from the Lord, the Spirit. (2 Cor 3:7–13)

This glory is glory only as it is kenotic:

For what we preach is not ourselves, but Jesus Christ as Lord,
with ourselves as your servants for Jesus' sake. For it is the God
who said, "Let light shine out of darkness," who has shone in our
hearts to give the light of the knowledge of the glory of God in
the face of Christ.

But we have this treasure in earthen vessels, to show that the
transcendent power belongs to God and not to us. . . . For while
we live we are always being given up to death for Jesus' sake, so
that the life of Jesus may be manifested in our mortal flesh. So
death is at work in us, but life in you. (2 Cor 4:5–7, 11–12)

Even as we engage kenosis, we are renewed:

So we do not lose heart. Though our outer nature is wasting
away [self-consciousness] our inner nature [deep mind] is being
renewed every day. For this slight momentary affliction is pre-
paring for us an eternal weight of glory beyond all comparison,
because we look not to the things that are seen but to the things
that are unseen; for the things that are seen are transient, but the
things that are unseen are eternal. (2 Cor 4:16–18)

The glory of kenosis transfigures us into a new creation. Note the emphatic *behold*:

"Therefore if anyone is in Christ, he is a new creation; the old has
passed away, *behold*, the new has come" (2 Cor 5:17). *Behold* occurs
twice early in the next chapter, summing up the reciprocity that has gone
before: "*Behold*, now is the acceptable time; *behold*, now is the day of

salvation (6:2b). And, ". . . as dying, and *behold* we live" (2 Cor 6:9). The latter passage constitutes another doxology, lining up the paradoxes:

> We are treated as imposters, and yet are true; as unknown, and yet well known; as dying, and behold we live; as punished, and yet not killed; as sorrowful, yet always rejoicing; as poor, yet making many rich; as having nothing, yet possessing everything. (2 Cor 6:8b–10)

Second Corinthians 8:9—"For you know the grace of our Lord Jesus Christ, that though he was rich, yet for your sake he became poor, so that by his poverty you might become rich"—is one of many examples of another apophatic trope: a sort of palindrome of meaning and effect, which is particularly prominent in the Gospels. Two classic examples are the stories of Dives and Lazarus (Luke 16:19–31) and the story of the healing of the man who was blind from birth in the Gospel of John (John 9). In the former, the meaning can be read in both directions: from a material and self-conscious point of view, Lazarus is poor and Dives is rich; on the other hand, according to the kingdom of God, Lazarus is rich and Dives is poor. The same inversion occurs in the story of the man blind from birth: he is blind according to a merely external point of view, while in these terms, the Pharisees can see. But according to the kingdom, it is the blind man who can see by faith even before he is cured; while the Pharisees remain blind. These sorts of inversions occur in many places in the Gospels. For example:

> And he called to him the multitude with his disciples, and said to them, "if any man would come after me, let him deny himself and take up his cross and follow me. For whoever would save his life will lose it; and whoever loses his life for my sake and the gospel's will save it." (Mark 8:34–38)

John Fenton is particularly eloquent on this passage in *Finding the Way through Mark*: ". . . salvation is through weakness, suffering, and being destroyed; . . . Salvation will not be by miraculous deliverance from evil, but by the destruction of the saviour, because anyone who saves his life will destroy it (12). The good news is not about life, but about life through death. (19)." To put this in terms of the model I have presented, to save your life, what is ostensibly life, that is, the self-conscious construction, but is in fact dead, is to remain in the self-conscious mind, which is derivative and whose thoughts are already rigid and narrow; while losing your life—the *kenosis* that elides self-consciousness and its constructs and delivers one into the kingdom of God, which is found in deep mind—is to save it. In fact, the entire theme of *kenosis* in the Bible is both paradox and palindrome. The two often go together, e.g., "seeing they do not see, and hearing they do not hear" (Matt 13:13); "whoever exalts himself will be humbled, and whoever humbles himself will be exalted" (Matt 23:11–12); "the last shall be first and the first last" (Luke 13:30); "No servant can serve two masters; for either he will hate the one and love the other, or he will be devoted to the one and despise the other. You cannot serve God and mammon" (Luke 16:13). The palindrome is an apophatic trope in the sense that the layers and resonances of meaning are too much for the receptive mind to take on board all at once and thus give it a moment of *quies*, of silence, which, if recognized, can be a gateway into deeper silence. We will return to the Gospels later in this chapter. In the meantime, we should repeat in passing that the word "glory" is itself apophatic as it dazzles the mind and opens it to unknowing.

Chapter 12 of Second Corinthians gives us another important paradox, evinced by Paul's "thorn in the flesh" (2 Cor 12:7–9). He reports that he has asked three times for it to be removed, but the Lord has said to him, "My grace is sufficient for you, for my power is made perfect in weakness." It is not by fixing our selves up that we receive the grace of God, but only by *kenosis* in accepting the form of our wounds. We might even say, paraphrasing and mirroring 1 Peter 2:24b: "Through our wounds we are healed," for it is precisely through our wounds that the grace of God enters us most freely and glorifies them in Christ's. As we noted earlier, the current fashion for talking about "true self" and "false self," as if we had to cut off bits of our selves to be acceptable to God, is entirely wrong.[5] We need *all* of our selves, warts and all, for our transfiguration in Christ. Nothing is lost; nothing is wasted. Finally, the paradox is reiterated in 2 Corinthians 13:4:

> For he was crucified in weakness, but lives by the power of God.
> For we are weak in him, but in dealing with you we shall live
> with him by the power of God.

---

5. As a matter of interest, it is equally considered a wrong view in Tibetan Buddhism. The construct of self in both Christianity and Buddhism, rather than being "destroyed," has no substantial reality of its own to begin with—it is a construct continually in flux. In Tibetan Buddhism, it belongs to the illusion that is "relative reality" rather than "ultimate reality." In Christianity, there is a parallel in the language of "the world" (or "the flesh") and "the kingdom of God."

First Peter expands this paradox in terms of glory, which leads us back to where we started:

> But rejoice in so far as you share Christ's sufferings, that you may also rejoice and be glad when his glory is revealed. If you are reproached for the name of Christ, you are blessed, because the Spirit of glory and of God rests upon you. (1 Pet 4:13–14)

The paradox is reiterated under various guises in 1 Peter: "So we do not lose heart . . ." (4:16); "For we know that if the earthly tent we live in is destroyed . . ." (5:1–4); "So we are always of good courage; we know that while we are at home in the body . . ." (5:6); "For we must all appear before the judgment seat of Christ . . ." (5:10).

———•———

This central paradox of *kenosis/glory-theosis* can be found throughout the New Testament; it reflects the psychological realities, the patterns of the mind we have explored in Volume 1. The beatitudes (Matt 5:3–11) are based on this paradox, and each counter-intuitive statement is an expression of refulgent glory:

> Blessed are the poor in spirit,[6] for theirs is the kingdom of heaven.
> Blessed are those who mourn, for they shall be comforted.
> Blessed are the meek for they shall inherit the earth.
> Blessed are those who hunger and thirst for righteousness, for they shall be satisfied.
> Blessed are the merciful, for they shall obtain mercy.
> Blessed are the pure in heart, for they shall see God.
> Blessed are the peacemakers, for they shall be called sons of God.
> Blessed are those who are persecuted for righteousness' sake, for theirs is the kingdom of heaven.
> Blessed are you when men revile you and persecute you and utter all kinds of evil against you falsely on my account. Rejoice and be glad, for your reward is great in heaven.

Each of the Beatitudes requires a kenotic movement. To know our need of God requires emptying out of our own sense of self-importance and self-sufficiency. Mourning empties a person out—at the bottom of mourning is a clean slate on which something new may be written.

———

6. The NEB has "How blest are those who know their need of God . . . ," which in my view is a much more illuminating translation. The first Beatitude would appear to be the source of Thérèse's "empty hands."

Meekness requires a kenotic attitude. Hungering and thirsting for righteousness means shedding all the pressures of "the world," i.e., political, social, and (particularly in John) religious systems. Mercy requires a relinquishing of power; purity of heart a single focus of attention. Peacemaking demands a refusal to impose on others; suffering persecution without retaliation is perhaps the closest to that of Jesus. All of these kenotic acts bring glory into the world, as expressed in the second half of each beatitude. And each of these kenotic acts bestows knowledge. Unsurprisingly, the words "glory" and "know" occur most often in the Gospel of John.

But in the Gospels, glory is also revealed in and through kenotic silence. It occurs in silence, and it causes silence, e.g., the healing miracles and Jesus' admonishments to keep silent about them.[7] They point away from themselves toward their purpose of giving and revealing glory manifested and celebrated in God. The onlookers are silenced before so great a mystery.

I find myself wondering if one reason that there are no resurrection stories—only the hint of resurrection in the empty tomb—in Mark is not only his appropriate reticence about the unsayable, but also that *the resurrection itself is like the miracles*: it isn't important in itself, spectacular though it is, but rather points (again) to the glory manifested and inherent by and in God through the ultimate kenosis of love, and to living the resurrected life in this world in all its glory in the midst of the world's destructiveness. The message is that if you have come to that stable identity in Christ, the wisdom that comes with self-forgetfulness and a calm abiding in deep mind, then you are incoercible, and while you may die for it, you have chosen to die for what you believe rather than what someone else imposes on you. Once you have come to that integrity, nothing else matters, not even crucifixion. As Pseudo-Dionysius remarks:

> [N]othing shall separate the one who believes in truth from the ground of true faith, and it is there that he will come into the possession of enduring, unchanging identity. The man in union with truth knows clearly that all is well with him even if everyone else thinks that he has gone out of his mind [Mark 3:21]. What they fail to see, naturally, is that he has gone out of the path of error and has in his real faith arrived at truth. He knows that far from being mad, as they imagine him to be, he has been rescued from the instability and the constant changes which

7. Fenton, *Finding the Way Through Mark*, 3.

bore him along the variety of error and that he has been set free by simple and immutable stable truth. This is why the principle leaders of our divine wisdom die each day for the truth. They bear witness in every word and deed to the single knowledge of the truth possessed by Christians. They prove that truth to be more simple and more divine than every other. Or, rather, what they show is that here is the only true, single, and simple knowledge of God. (DN 872D–873A)[8]

In reading through the Gospel of Mark, I found thirty-four instances of silence of different kinds. I suspect that more could be found using a more subtle and expansive interpretation from the Greek. But here is a tentative list:

- silence of the wilderness (by implication) (1:12); also, Jesus binds Satan (by implication—Satan's temptations are noise; Jesus silences him) (3:27);

- silences demon (1:25); silences demons (1:34, 39);

- goes to a lonely place (implicit silence) (1:35);

- commands healed leper to be silent (1:44);

- people in synagogue are silent when Jesus asks if it is lawful to do good on the Sabbath (3:4);

- Jesus silences unclean spirits (3:12);[9]

- he who has ears to hear, let him hear (4:9);

- "Silence! Be still!" (spoken to the sea) (4:39);

- woman touches his garment in silence (implicit) (5:27–29);

- tells Jairus and wife not to tell of the raising of their daughter (5:43);

- goes up alone on the mountain to pray (6:46);

- the sick touch his garment (implicit silence) (6:56b);

- (quoting Isaiah) "teaching as doctrines the precepts of men" (implicit is the idea that God's word comes out of silence) (7:7);

- healing the man who is deaf and dumb—he charged them to tell no one (7:36);

- healing of blind man (8:26);

8. *Pseudo-Dionysius: Complete Works*, 110.

9. John Fenton believes it is not possible to speak clearly about that which is not clear, and he does not try to do so (*Finding the Way*, 25).

- "do not tell that I am the Messiah" (8:30);

- transfiguration (9:2–8); silences Peter, James, and John not to talk about the transfiguration (9:9);

- Jesus doesn't want people to know where he is going because he is teaching the disciples (prediction of his death and resurrection) (9:30);

- crowd tell Bartimeus to be quiet but he won't (10:48);

- Jesus won't tell the chief priests, scribes, and elders who he is (silences them; glory is self-evident for those who can see, as in many of the examples that follow) (11:33);

- the stone which the builders rejected (12:10);

- no one dared to ask him any questions (12:34);

- "stay awake" (vigilance requires silence) (13:32–37); to disciples in Gethsemane to "stay awake" (14:34); the same after they are found sleeping (14:36); the disciples fall silent when he finds them asleep; there is no relief from desolation (14:40);[10]

- silence before the high priest (14:61); he does not respond when mocked and told to prophesy (14:65); silence before Pilate (15:5); silence before the mockers (15:18–20);

- silence of tomb (15:46);

- silence of the women at the tomb who did not obey the young man and report to the disciples (16:8).

Mark is perhaps the most kenotic and ironic of the Gospels. As John Fenton remarks, "The Parable of the Sower and the different kinds of ground illustrates what Mark believes to be the fundamental gospel-truth, that gain is through loss, success through failure, salvation through destruction, and life through death."[11] This theme is emphasized again and again in *Finding the Way through Mark* in uncompromising terms:

> Everybody who wants to be a follower of his [Jesus] must embrace destruction. They must stop working for their own good, and making that the motive for their existence. To renounce self means to disown one's self, to dissociate one's self from the claims that the self makes. It is the same word that will be used of Peter saying that he does not know Jesus. In the end, these are the only alternatives that we have: to disown yourself, or

10. Fenton, *Finding the Way*, 99.
11. Ibid., 23.

to disown Christ. Peter will choose the second, Jesus must the first. (The teaching that is being given here assumes that human beings have this extraordinary ability to transcend themselves, and distinguish between the I that observes and the me that is observed. There will be no let-up in the conflict between these two.) . . .

The underlying principle is then stated with brutal clarity: attempting to save your life is in fact self-destruction, but self-destruction is salvation. Not all self-destruction; only when it is for the sake of Jesus and for the sake of the gospel.

The requirement of death and the promise of resurrection stand side by side, neither diminishing the other. Death must be total giving, as though there were nothing to come after; and resurrection must be the completely gratuitous action of God, concerning which we may not presume.[12]

Fenton's language of self-destruction (self-emptying) is extreme, but we must remember that he was deeply affected by the harsh von Hugel language and psychological misunderstandings of his day. Underneath the harshness, however, he is talking about the move from self-consciousness to deep mind, and the repentance this entails. In another *Repent* place, he remarks that within the hyperbole of Mark's dark message, all that is needed for salvation is faith and repentance:

(. . . Gain comes through loss, and salvation through destruction.) To accept the good news of God, all that is needed is repentance and faith, changing one's mind from the way human beings think [self-consciousness], and believing that what seems impossible is in fact the way God works. . . .[13] History is a downhill progress, and God intervenes when the lowest level has been reached.[14] . . . [S]alvation is through weakness, suffering, and being destroyed. . . . Salvation will not be by miraculous deliverance from evil, but by the destruction of the saviour, because anyone who saves his life will destroy it.[15] The good news is not about life, but about life through death.[16]

The requirement of death and the promise of resurrection stand side by side, neither diminishing the other. Death must be total giving, as though there were nothing to come after; and

12. Ibid., 50–51.
13. Ibid., 9.
14. Ibid., 10.
15. Ibid., 12.
16. Ibid., 19.

resurrection must be the completely gratuitous action of God, concerning which we may not presume.[17]

The gospel is biased in favour of the wicked; the advantage they have is that they will be more likely to repent. The problem with the law, as Paul had found, is that one might keep it, and that would make repentance unnecessary.[18]

⸺•⸺

The Gospel of Matthew is full of similar silences, paradoxes, and palindromes, which is unsurprising, given that the Synoptics have texts in common. Silence is often indicative and/or inclusive of paradox and palindromes. Paradox and what is merely counter-intuitive are difficult to distinguish from one another and perhaps it does not matter, for the end result is the same: the mind's usual chatter is silenced for a moment and a new perspective opens up. In Matthew there are also the silences that issue from beholding of angels, that is, one of the means by which God communicates himself in the world. In chapters 1–3 they appear five times:

- angel appears to Joseph telling him that Mary is pregnant by the Holy Spirit (1:20);

- dream warns wise men (angel is implicit) (2:12);

- angel appears to Joseph telling him to flee to Egypt (2:13);

- angel appears to Joseph telling him to return to Israel (2:19);

- angels minister to Jesus in the desert (4:11).

(We may also note the voice from heaven at Jesus' baptism (3:17).) Often the statements in Matthew and the other Gospels entail silence without explicitly expressing it, e.g., give alms in secret (6:2); pray in secret (6:6); fast in secret seen only by your Father in heaven, who is secret (6:16–17); woman with hemorrhage touches his garment (in silence) (9:20, also 14:36); command to healed blind men not to tell anyone (silence) (9:30); Jesus goes to a lonely place and to a mountain to pray— silence is implicit (14:13 and 14:23). It is also implicit in the account of the glory of Transfiguration (17:1–10) and the doxology that precedes the narrative at the end of 16:27–28.

17. Ibid., 52.
18. Ibid., 16.

After the vision has faded (17:9), Jesus overtly commands Peter, James, and John not to speak of what they have seen (in silence), that is, not to trivialize or domesticate the unspeakable glory that they have beheld—a rebuke to Peter who in his terror has indeed spoken in the silence (17:4), and made the ridiculous suggestion that the disciples should materialize and claim the glory by building three booths for Jesus, Moses, and Elijah. This was a way of distracting from the light he could not bear. Icons often show the disciples shielding their eyes from the face of Jesus which "shone like the sun, and his garments became white as light" (17:2) and here Peter is speaking out of spiritual blindness. The voice from heaven (17:5) is apophatic, and when Jesus finally speaks to the disciples to tell them not to fear, the moment of transfiguration has passed (17:7–8).

In 21:23–27, Jesus silences the elders; in 22:23–34, he silences the Sadducees. In 22:41–46, he silences the Pharisees once again. And then there are Jesus's own silences: he is silent before the high priest (26:63); he is silent when abused (26:67–68); he is silent before Pilate (27:12, 14); he is silent while being mocked (27:27–30); he is silent on the cross (27:39–44).

Luke's mythologizing is also full of silences, paradoxes, and palindromes of meaning, some of which are shared with the other Gospels, and some which are unique. Each of the tropes leads to silence or plunges the reader into a moment of silence. What follows is not exhaustive; I have tried to cite instances that are of special interest. There is the barren silence of Elizabeth in 1:7; the silence of the temple where Zechariah is offering incense in 1:9; in 1:20 the angel tells Zechariah he will be silent and in 1:22 he emerges mute, unable to speak for the whole of Elizabeth's pregnancy. In 1:28 there is the silence of the place where Mary received Gabriel—in fact, all appearances of angels are implicitly in the context of silence, and while they "speak" it is communication through silence.

There is the silence of the wilderness where John the Baptist roams (1:80); in 2.8 the silence of the shepherds' fields; in 2:16 the silence of the manger; in 4:2 the silence of forty days in the wilderness. In 4:35 and 4:41 Jesus tells demons to be silent—it is interesting that demons are often associated with noise, not only in the Gospels but also in the accounts of the hermits of the desert, as, for example, Anthony being attacked by demons in his solitude. In 17:12 there is the silence of the death of the son of the widow of Nain; silence is implicit in 8:8b, "he who has ears to hear, let him hear"; in 8:10 the disciples are to know the secrets of the kingdom; in 10:39 we find Mary's silence, listening at the feet of the Lord.

As noted elsewhere, the word "behold" not only implies silence in the narrative but also silences the reader. It occurs three times in Luke 17:21, which could be said to be one of the most important passages in the Bible from the point of view of this book. This is a composite translation referencing the Greek:

> Being asked by the Pharisees when the kingdom of God was coming, he answered them, "The kingdom of God is not coming with signs to be observed, nor will they say, 'Behold, here it is!' or 'Behold there it is,' for behold, the kingdom of God is within you."

This passage is particularly pertinent to our days when there are many people claiming to have the secret of the kingdom of heaven, though they don't always use that language. This situation reminds us of the "signs and wonders" passage in the Gospel of John, "Unless you see signs and wonders you will not believe" (John 4:48), and the "itching ears" passage in 2 Timothy 4:3–4:

> For the time is coming when people will not endure sound teaching, but having itching ears they will accumulate for themselves teachers to suit their own likings, and will turn away from listening to the truth and will wander into myths.

All of these passages are in the background of the statement by Abba Moses, the desert father, "Go and sit in your cell, and your cell will teach you everything." Good Buddhist teachers have a similar approach. They will often say, "Do not believe me, but experience this for yourself." Language is dangerous: it can convey insight, to be sure, but ultimately divine knowledge for the most part is communicated in silence and solitude. As Psalm 19:1–4 says,

> The heavens declare the glory of God, and the firmament shows his handiwork.
> One day tells its tale to another, and one night imparts knowledge to another.
> Although they have no words or language, and their voices are not heard,
> Their sound has gone out into all lands, and their message to the ends of the earth. (1979 BCP)

To explore thoroughly the passages in the Gospel of John that illustrate inversions, silence, kenosis, and glory would fill up another book. John is the gospel that doesn't just *talk about* the glory of God, beholding, and the kingdom of heaven, it *manifests* it. As we already have seen, Jesus speaks of his indwelling with the disciples, and his glory that he shares with them from the Father. There is no talk of secret teaching in John, quite the reverse: "Jesus answered him, 'I have spoken openly in the world; I have always taught in synagogues and in the temple. . . . I have said nothing secretly'" (John 18:20).

If Ephesians is the epistle of glory, then John is the gospel of glory. In fact, it is almost an essay on glory in fragmentary form. It is worth going through the relevant passages one at a time, to see how they are interrelated and form a whole. The word search and quotations in what follows are from the NRSV.

"And the Word became flesh and lived among us, and we have seen (beheld) his glory, the glory as of a father's only son, full of grace and truth" (John 1:14). The prologue clearly announces the purpose of this gospel, which is to manifest glory, the glory that Jesus the Christ both teaches and manifests with the *kenosis* of his life.

"Jesus did this, the first of his signs, in Cana of Galilee, and revealed his glory; and his disciples believed in him" (John 2:11). Jesus obeys his mother's request even though he feels that his hour is not yet come, even though the kenotic act of turning water into wine foreshadows the spilling of his blood in the passion. This is his first kenotic act in John's Gospel.

"I do not accept glory from human beings" (John 5:41). Here Jesus makes a sharp distinction between the glory that human beings try to accrue for themselves, and the divine glory that is kenotic. He reiterates the point in 5:44: "How can you believe when you accept glory from one another and do not seek the glory that comes from the one who alone is God?" And again in 7:18: "Those who speak on their own seek their own glory; but the one who seeks the glory of him who sent him is true, and there is nothing false in him." And again in 8:50: "Yet I do not seek my own glory; there is one who seeks it and he is the judge;" and 8:54: Jesus answered, "If I glorify myself, my glory is nothing. It is my Father who glorifies me, he of whom you say, 'He is our God.'"

Combined with the "signs and wonders" and "itching ears" passages quoted above, it becomes clear that the problem of celebrity gurus was as big a problem in Jesus' day as it is in ours, and not confined to Christianity. As Tosknyi Rinpoche, a contemporary Tibetan Buddhist teacher puts it:

> We tell ourselves that we need some spirituality in our lives, that we can't be totally materialistic. So we give ourselves a little dose [of spiritual practice] in the morning and evening to give the gloss of spirituality to our normal life. This is also a particular solution or style, and certain teachers—not masters, but teachers—teach in this way. They instruct their students in five-minute meditation sessions. They are trying to make spiritual practice more easy, more appetizing or palatable; trying to bend the Dharma to fit people's attitudes. That is not the true Dharma. It is possible that we could encounter this type of "convenience-Dharma" when we go back to our own countries. Don't make the mistake of confusing this type of practice for the real thing.[19]

The theme of *kenosis*/glory recurs in the story of Lazarus: "But when Jesus heard it, he said, 'This illness does not lead to death; rather it is for God's glory, so that the Son of God may be glorified through it'" (11:4). The raising of Lazarus is costly. In 11:33–44 the NRSV falls on its face. It says Jesus was "deeply moved" twice. The KJV rather emphasizes the costliness—both personally and politically—to Jesus of raising Lazarus. He twice "groans in the spirit. The insipid NRSV conveys nothing of the costliness of Jesus' agony in the raising of Lazarus, which foreshadows the agony of his passion and crucifixion.

In 11:40 Jesus says, "Did I not tell you that if you believed, you would see the glory of God?" Belief, too, can be costly, and Martha's belief and earlier declaration of faith (11:21–27) are kenotic.

John emphasizes the theme of glory especially as Jesus moves towards his passion and death. In 12:23, he says: Jesus answered them, "The hour has come for the Son of Man to be glorified," even though, we have been told in 12:16 that, "His disciples did not understand this [i.e., Jesus' entry into Jerusalem] at first; but when Jesus was glorified, then they remembered that this had been written of him and had been done to him." That *kenosis* is glory is reiterated in 12:28: "Father, glorify your name." Then a voice came from heaven, "I have glorified it, and I will glorify it

19. Tsoknyi Rinpoche, *Carefree Dignity*, 135–36.

again." Once again Jesus points away from himself in 12:30: "This voice has come for your sake, not for mine."

Towards the end of the chapter, in 12:41, speaking of those who reject Jesus, John links Jesus to Isaiah 10, and comments, "Isaiah said this because he saw his glory and spoke about him." He continues, "Nevertheless many, even of the authorities, believed in him. But because of the Pharisees they did not confess it, for fear that they would be put out of the synagogue; for they loved human glory more than the glory that comes from God." The desire is there, but it is not great enough to overcome *Kenotic* reluctance to pay the kenotic price, echoing, perhaps, Matthew 26:41 *Price* (NRSV): "The spirit indeed is willing, but the flesh is weak."

This cowardice is implicitly contrasted with Jesus' willingness to undergo his passion. After Judas' departure to betray him, Jesus says in John 13:31–32: "Now the Son of Man has been glorified, and God has been glorified in him. If God has been glorified in him, God will also glorify him in himself and will glorify him at once." The theme continues in the next few chapters: "I will do whatever you ask in my name, so that the Father may be glorified in the Son" (14:13:); "My Father is glorified by this, that you bear much fruit and become my disciples" (15:8). In other words, the disciples should practice the *kenosis* they have been taught by Jesus so that they may manifest the Father's glory. This is reiterated in 16:14: "He [the Spirit] will glorify me, because he will take what is mine and declare it to you."

John 17:5, 10, 22, and 24 confirm the sharing of the kenotic glory of the Father and Son—and implicitly the Spirit to come—with the disciples. "So now, Father, glorify me in your own presence with the glory that I had in your presence before the world existed" (v. 5); "All mine are yours, and yours are mine; and I have been glorified in them" (v. 10); "The glory that you have given me I have given them, so that they may be one, as we are one" (v. 22); "Father, I desire that those also, whom you have given me, may be with me where I am, to see my glory, which you have given me because you loved me before the foundation of the world" (v. 24). Finally, there is the scene with Peter, which is at once poignant and touching, and a passage of joy. Jesus asks Peter three times if he loves him and then tells him of his death: "(He said this to indicate the kind of death by which he would glorify God.) After this he said to him, 'Follow me'" (21:19).

From start to finish, the Gospel of John is about glory, in stark contrast to the Gospel of Mark with its silences and secrets. Or perhaps

John is the deliberate obverse of the Gospel of Mark: an expansion and manifestation of the glory that was previously concealed. As we saw in the previous volume there is much to link the two gospels. Searching each gospel book with the syllable "glor" in the NRSV there are five occurrences in Mark, seven in Matthew, sixteen in Luke, but, although all the Gospels speak of *kenosis* as praxis in parables and gesture towards glory, none of the Synoptics is as specific as John—twenty-eight occurrences—and none use the notion as apophatically as John nor as overtly as his account of the essence of the message of Jesus. Nor are any of the Synoptics so thoroughly linked thematically as John in picking up the threads of the Epistles, which were written before them. Glory is the message of the New Testament: it dominates the Epistles, and it is explored clearly by John and more indirectly by the Synoptics.

There has long been a faction in Christianity and in biblical studies that has claimed that Paul "ruined" the message of Jesus. Perhaps we should consider rather that Paul understood very well what is the message of Jesus, and that it is the Synoptics that dilute the message, while John picks it up and gives it both its fullest and most apophatic, as well as its most practical exposition.

FOUR

Liturgical Silence

The highest form of praise is silence.

—St Ephrem[1]

The modern habit of doing ceremonial things unceremoniously is no proof of humility; rather it proves the offender's inability to forget himself in the rite, and his readiness to spoil for every one else the proper pleasure of ritual.

—C. S. Lewis[2]

I feel the real medium for me is silence, so I could be writing in any language. To inflect the inner silence, to give it body, that's all we're doing. You use the voice to make the silence present. The real subject in poetry isn't the voice. The real subject is silence.

—Li Young Lee[3]

"The priests are still and the deacons stand in silence, the whole people is quiet and still, subdued and calm; . . . the mysteries are set in order, the censers are smoking, the lamps are shining, and the deacons are hovering and brandishing [fans] in the likeness of the Watchers. Deep silence and peaceful calm settles on that place; it

1. Quoted in Brock, *Luminous Eye*, 79.
2. Lewis, *A Preface to Paradise Lost*, 16.
3. Lee, "The Subject is Silence," 121.

*is filled and overflows with brightness and splendour, beauty and
power."... [T]he consecration is the moment of resurrection, another
remarkable link to the royal traditions of Israel, for the king was
deemed to be resurrected (translated "raised up," 2 Sam 23.1) and
he too became the Lord enthroned and he too was worshipped (1 Chr
29:20–23, the Lord with his people).*

—MARGARET BARKER, QUOTING THE SONGS OF THE SABBATH SACRI-
FICE[4]

THE TITLE OF THIS chapter is more than ironic, for if there is one aspect
that is lacking in modern liturgy, it is silence, and without silence, there
is no going beyond self-consciousness. In the cathedral where I worship,
the deacon often comes out before the Eucharist begins and says, "We
will now have silence to prepare ourselves." Instead of a cathedral-sized
silence ensuing, the organ immediately starts to play. When I mentioned
this to someone they remarked rather sarcastically, "We pay the organist
a lot of money; we need to use his services." I have a feeling that this cleric
had tried to bring up the topic of silence and had been rebuffed by the
powers that be, most of whom are terrified of silence.

Also missing, and related to silence proper is poetry, which, as Li
Young Lee says in the epigraph above, in the end is not about words, but
about silence. In fact, as we saw in the first volume, poetry requires us to
use both parts of our mind. Yet we have taken all the poetry out of the
liturgy, the most effective way to use language to move us into deep mind.
Most of the present-day liturgies and translations of the Bible are simply
awful. They are clunky and insipid; they lack any sense of beauty and
mystery; for the most part, they do not translate the word "behold," which
occurs in both ancient Hebrew and Greek and is essential to the meaning
of the texts. Some passages of the NRSV are so awkward that they have
the effect of listening to someone falling down the stairs. Or consider the
acclamation at the fraction, the ceremonial act of breaking the eucharistic bread, which in the Church of England could not be more banal or
infantile: "Though we are many, we are one body, because we all share

---

4. In Barker, *The Great High Priest*, 67–68. The Songs of the Sabbath Sacrifice is a
text that was composed around 100 BCE and was widely known in its day.

in one bread." The fraction is the climax of the liturgy: by this time the worshippers should have been moved beyond the symbols into the deep mind. Such a banality yanks the worshipper back into self-consciousness; instead, there should be silence. If there has to be an acclamation, let it be, "Christ our Passover is sacrificed for us: therefore let us keep the feast." The fraction mirrors the "therefore" in Philippians 2:5–11, which is not magic, but a space of opportunity; a space where transfiguration and resurrection take place, and, as we have noted elsewhere, it is like a cosmic intake of breath that contains infinite potential and resurrection.

Catholics complain vociferously about the terrible translation of their liturgy, but at least it has restored "and with your spirit" to replace the truly dire "and also with you," which, as Madeleine L'Engle used to say over and over, implicitly demands a further response of "likewise I'm sure." We need to completely revise our liturgies from scratch, using the criteria of what we are trying to evoke from our worship as our guide, and taking into consideration what we know about the way the mind works to effect it.

First, liturgy has or should have an arc that moves us from self-consciousness to self-forgetfulness. Present-day liturgy does anything but. There are constant interruptions that throw us back into our self-consciousness: repeated breast-beating; the Creed(s)—there should be no place in liturgy for propositional political compromises; the non-stop prolixity; too many readings; contradictory theologies. The clergy never shut up, and never stop drawing attention to themselves; they should rather be effacing themselves to focus on the Eucharist. Related to this is the failure to understand the goal of liturgy, which is transfiguration. Here is Hilarion Alfeyev reflecting on Isaac the Syrian's comments about the night vigil, which has the same effect on the worshipper as eucharistic liturgy properly celebrated:

> "For night vigil is the light of the thinking (*tar'ita*); and by it the understanding (*mad'a*) is exalted, the mind (*re'yana*) is collected, and the intellect (*hauna*) takes flight and gazes at spiritual things and by prayer is rejuvenated and shines brightly." This passage is unique in Isaac in that he uses together all four Syriac terms relative to the mental faculties of the human person. By doing so, Isaac probably wants to emphasize that night prayer can embrace an entire person and totally transfigure the person's whole intellectual sphere. Nocturnal prayer has, in Isaac, an all-embracing character and is regarded as a universal means

for attaining illumination of mind. . . . Transfiguration of the
mind, purification of the heart, and mystical vision of God, are
the fruits of night vigil.[5]

Maximus the Confessor, according to Jaroslav Pelikan, agrees:

"Who knows," Maximus asked, "how God is made flesh and yet
remains God?" And he answered his own question: "This only
faith understands, adoring the Logos in silence." It was then a
genuine understanding, but one that appropriately expressed
itself "in silence" rather than in words. Not even the words of
the orthodox dogma, for which Maximus contended and suf-
fered all his life, could adequately encompass the mystery of
faith. "Theological mystagogy" transcended the dogmas for-
mulated by the councils for the Church. A spirituality shaped
by orthodox apophaticism, therefore, was one that gratefully
acknowledged those dogmas and was ready to defend them to
the death against those who sought to distort them, but that, at
the same time, willingly—in fact, worshipfully—acknowledged
the limitations that had been placed on all knowledge and all
affirmation, be it human or angelic. . . . [W]orship [is] the appropriate modality for knowing the unknowable and expressing
the inexpressible.[6]

But the Eucharist is more than a personal or even communal transfiguration. It is a gathering—of the fragments of our selves into whole-
ness in the deep mind; of the fragmented members of the congregation
into communion at every level, of the fragments of our day-to-day living
into some sort of coherent pattern. The detritus of self-image is, or should
be, shed to reveal naked humanity, which, through the Eucharist, puts
on the robe of glory. As we saw in the last volume, it was Paschasius'
emphasis on the material elements on the altar and their place in time
as opposed to the liturgical movement and the mingling of heaven and
earth in timelessness that led to narcissism and magical clergy power-
plays in worship. This was a huge category mistake, moving from the
perceptual to the virtual, from outward and kenotic to inward and narcis-
sistic. Paschasius closed the Eucharist so that it is no longer a vehicle of
trans-figuration, but rather a repetitive linear feedback loop, a plaything
of the clergy, and a denigration of the laity. "This is my body" became the
magical thinking of so-called transubstantiation, rather than self-offering

5. Alfeyev, *The Spiritual World*, 192.
6. Introduction to Bertold (ed.), *Maximus the Confessor*, 9.

prayed in the heart with the community and communal understanding—in every sense—of "you in me and I in you and we in the Father." We must always guard against a tendency to descend into religious practice instead of ascending into the incarnation of our full humanity.

Doctrine was originally a series of metaphors for talking about the properties of the mind. In the early church, there was still a linking of mind and heart (as per Jewish ways of looking at it). When Jesus and Paul talk about the "foolishness of the wise" (1 Cor 1:27) they aren't kidding, they aren't being metaphorical. They're talking about the simplicity of the work of silence and the simplification that takes place with the work of silence. What is "divine" (as Nicholas of Cusa also says much later) is the mysteriousness of the mind, the fact, for example, that the greater part of the mind is directly (though not indirectly) inaccessible, and that it is able to make transfigurative changes in the person that the self-conscious mind can't. In addition, it is also able to be kenotic to the point of *excessus mentis*, which is the essence of the great commandment to love God, neighbor, and self with a single self-forgetful love. Eucharist can be seen as "physically you [fellow-worshippers, Christ, the Father] share in the spirit of my life now; when I am out of sight, this is a substitute tangible way for you to share in my spirit" to engage us in this great commandment. As J. P. Williams notes, "The Christian's apophatic awareness of God finds him more perfectly expressed in the movements of the liturgy [Pseudo-Dionysius] than in words, and in the individual's moral life as much as her theology."[7]

Liturgy is often spoken of as theater or drama, but the danger here is that if it gets too theatrical it becomes artificial and camp. Perhaps what is meant is something like this: when you go to a theater, a "place of beholding," you lose your self-consciousness in your absorption in the drama, dipping in and out of *excessus mentis*. As Aristotle says, tragedy provides a purgation of the emotions—the emotions themselves aren't purified so much as elided—leaving the beholder in a state of inner silence, which might look like numbness but is quite the reverse, an awed compassion.[8] The point is that the tragedy is doing its work—is giving pleasure—on a

---

7. J. P. Williams, *Denying Divinity*, 10.

8. Ringu Tulku Rinpoche, in a talk on 15 May 2017, suggested that genuine compassion is not "suffering with" as it is usually interpreted in the West. It does no one good if the one having compassion becomes part of the problem. Rather, he suggested that genuine compassion was an empathy that wished for—and enabled as far as possible—the other to be free from whatever was troubling him or her, which is quite a different proposition.

level far below self-consciousness, which is suspended in beholding. In other words, one doesn't watch a tragedy self-consciously thinking "What jolly fun!" Rather, all the thinking, and the entire point of the art form, rests on the simultaneous and mutually-implicating working of rational thought and elision of emotion somewhere in the deep mind, to create a great silence.

All God has ever asked of us is to behold, and all the church is required to do is to enable that beholding by teaching us how to *listen* at the deepest level so that the gate to deep mind is always open and the divine wellspring informs our daily living. This immersing of us in mystery through theater means that any good liturgist worth his or her salt will incorporate alterations of light and darkness, silence and language, set up semiotic resonances and words knots, and rhythms that go beneath the level of speech; these subtleties will not be lost on the worshiper: even a baby knows how to enter the mystery of playing peek-a-boo.

But liturgy should not infantilize, and this tendency is one of the main reasons that people are leaving the churches in droves. They do not feel as though they are taken seriously as adults, as "full Christians." In my experience, it is the rule, not the exception, that clergy regard their congregations as bums in pews that are sources of money and little else. At one parish I briefly attended, every Sunday at the main Eucharist there were pieces of paper in each pew demanding that worshippers give money, time, or talent. From the point of view of the worshipper, this exploitive and preoccupying request overshadowed the entire liturgy so that relinquishing self-consciousness became impossible. By contrast, here is Jane Hirshfield. She is talking about speaking and writing poetry, but what she says applies to the effect liturgy should have on us: ". . . to stand humbled and stunned and silent before the wild and inexplicable beauties and mysteries of being."[9] What she says about writers on the threshold applies to every worshipper:

> The heart that knows there is nothing to look for beyond this moment will accept them all. . . . [Such a heart] will laugh with everyone, welcome everyone. . . . Whatever [and whoever] wants to enter such a heart will be allowed to enter.
>
> It is the task of the writer to become that permeable and transparent; to become, in the words of Henry James, a person on whom nothing is lost. What is put into the care of such a person will be well tended, . . . [she will] tell the stories she is

9. Hirshfield, *Nine Gates*, 221.

given . . . with the compassion that comes when the self's deepest interest is not in the self, but in turning outward and into
awareness.[10]

I could go on *ad nauseam* about what is wrong with our liturgies;
many other writers have done so at length replete with elegant scholarship and myriad suggestions for alteration. But all the scholarship in the
world is not going to help us create liturgies that move us along the trajec-
tory from self-consciousness to deep mind, from language to apophasis.
Nor am I going to suggest designer liturgies in theory—we have had far
too many designer liturgies, too much theory and not enough praxis.

What I *am* going to do, however, is to present a liturgy that is designed to expose the roots of Eucharist, from which, perhaps, other liturgies might arise. It is designed to change perspective on the liturgy, and
the perspectives of those who celebrate liturgy.

---

10. Hirshfield, *Nine Gates*, 223.

Excursus:

A Rite for Contemplative Eucharist

Contents

Introduction

The purpose of this rite is reconciliation. It restores the Eucharist to the people of God; it offers an opportunity for the clergy to learn to trust the laity. It has the capacity to give everyone who participates, clergy and laity alike, an opportunity to understand more fully what it means to be "a reasonable, holy, and living sacrifice, acceptable to God."

This rite creates a minimal liturgical structure in which participants may discover that the Eucharist is not an object or objects over which magic words have been said by a remote cleric, but rather that the Eucharist is the gathering of every moment of each of our lives, of the life of all creation, all our pain and sorrow, all our laughter and joy gathered into a single timeless moment in which Christ is revealed to inhere, to have been present, to be present now, to be forever present. It makes available in an existential way the knowledge that not only are we beloved of God as we are, but also that nothing, absolutely nothing can separate us from the love of God, and that nothing in our lives is ever wasted.

But the full meaning of Eucharist lies in the heart, beyond language, concept, and time. The rite provides a context in which each participant may consciously live Eucharist in silence. Each person's interpretation will be differently nuanced, and each person's silence must be respected and encouraged by the depth of silence of those animating the rite, as well as those participating in it.

While this rite grows out of the Anglican tradition, it is suitable for use by any group wishing to deepen their lives in God. The guidelines below include practical suggestions for groups without clergy as well as those having more "Catholic" limitations.

That we *are* Eucharist is inherent in the theology behind Cranmer's rather awkward rite in which the worshippers receive Communion immediately after the words of institution. Cranmer is, of course, drawing on a much earlier patristic tradition. Realizing our union in Christ, being en-Christed—that is, realizing union with God, our neighbor, and ourselves as a single union in love—is the "medicine of life," to use a favorite metaphor of the early church. The words "this is my body" should sound in our hearts referring to our own flesh and blood, the totality of our lives, equally as we hear it sounded from and meaning Christ, for it is Christ indwelling we offer, Christ who offers himself without end.

While this rite is particularly effective for catechumens, for those who often feel unacceptable or are shunned by or isolated from society, e.g., the sick, especially those with AIDS, prisoners, the elderly, and for those in need of reconciliation, its use is not confined to these groups or these contexts. It has been used for a decade in parishes from remote Alaska to suburban London.

This rite also offers a corrective. Over the centuries, the view that the Eucharist belongs to the clergy has undermined the confidence of the laity in their approach to God, and has created an abyss between them and the clergy. This rite bridges that abyss. It enables people to begin to come to the altar—whether the physical altar or the altar of their hearts—with *parrhesia*, with a confidence that arises from true humility, as opposed to the alienation that arises from humiliation. It returns the role of the clerical hierarchy (if clergy are present) to a more appropriate kenotic balance. If the ordained participate in this rite with an open heart their vocation can be renewed and transfigured. For some people the rite has proved not only life-enhancing but permanently life-changing at every level.

There is always a danger in writing down a rite that came into being as a gift. It is possible that it may lose its spontaneity, that it may become fossilized, used in an inappropriate way, or exploited as just another "spiritual" consumer item. But the situation in the churches has become so dire that the time has come to set these reservations aside and make it generally available.

The rite itself teaches us that nothing can go "wrong" in the liturgy, that everything that happens to us and everything we do within its context is liturgy and acceptable to God, for liturgy is life. The non-ordained people of God have an innate liturgical sense, and giving them the opportunity to exercise it can help the clergy understand how to help them on the way, to relax the strictures that often make liturgical celebrations anything but contemplative and anything but celebratory. It can remove a huge burden of stress from clerical lives as well as expanding the vision and understanding of the laity.

History

The rite first came into being in 1995 in an Episcopal church in Cincinnati in the Diocese of Southern Ohio when I was Theologian in Residence.

---

1. Kenosis at the simplest level means self-emptying, the decreasing awareness of oneself that occurs naturally as one focuses with increasing intensity on something else.

My schedule for the five weeks was far too full, and the words "Workshop in Contemplative Prayer" which appeared on my timetable for a Saturday were a very welcome sight. The only problem was the title, which seemed self-refuting. While some spiritual writers may talk about "the work of contemplation," it is rather working at not working, or, it is working to stop working and simply be.

As the day approached, I found it impossible to plan it in the ordinary sense. There was an intuition that it would involve Eucharist, so the parish where it was to be held was asked to lay in a large supply of standard issue "priest's" hosts (the fish food variety about three inches in diameter) if they didn't already have them.

At 9:45 AM on the appointed day I arrived to find the church basement filled with about fifty people in casual dress, chatting and eating doughnuts, and drinking coffee. The atmosphere was ordinary, congenial. The oldest person was approaching ninety years of age and the youngest was twelve years old. This scene of people enjoying and reverencing one another in their ordinariness was itself Eucharist. Anything we did would be an extension of it.

I still had no specific plan—I seemed prevented, somehow, from making one. But at least there would be an introduction and silence together, so we began by rearranging the chairs.

To describe what happened after we began is very difficult. It was as if we had somehow entered a timeless space that opened out and embraced us. As each part of the rite was set into motion, the next part presented itself as if it had been waiting for us from eternity. It was an extraordinary day, and it would have been a mistake to try to repeat it, but the form of the rite was given and over time has proved enduring.

On that particular occasion, by the time the rite proper was finished and people were sitting quietly in the church making their thanksgivings, we had been more than four hours in silence. When the last person—the rector—left his seat in the nave, nearly five hours had passed. If nothing else, this day proved that the degree to which the laity will be receptive to silence and unafraid of it is the degree to which those who animate the rites in which they participate are receptive to silence and unafraid of it. Furthermore, the laity seek after such silence but are too often inhibited by their clergy, who think the laity are "not ready" for it, when it is themselves who are not ready.

One of the very few requests made of participants at the beginning of this rite is that when it is over they do not talk about what has happened with anyone, not with each other, not with their families, not with the animator, not with the clergy. It is also suggested that participants try to live out of the silence of the day at least interiorly, if not exteriorly, for as long as possible. The reason for these requests is to forestall "evaluations" that might dissipate the energy of the deep communion that has been realized, or trivialize by concept what lies beyond words and linear thought. There is no "success" or "failure" to this rite; it is our life in God, flawed as that may be, no more, no less.

Of course there is always someone who, in spite of the request not to talk about it, will come afterwards and say, "I know I'm not supposed to talk about this, but . . ." It is important for the animator (or whoever is listening to these words) to receive these communications gratefully but neutrally; to want not to know. It is not that the listener does not respect what has happened to the participant, but rather that the listener ought to respect it so profoundly that it's none of his or her business.

To animate this rite can be perilous to the soul of the animator. If one is to stay empty enough to facilitate it there is absolutely no room for self-congratulation or for the mind-set that entertains words such as "achievement." The animator must attempt to have the same profound focus as in formal sitting or walking meditation, not only during the rite and in its preparation, but as an expression of a way of life, so that the silence communicated from the outset is not an artificial silence or an imposed silence, but a shared silence of being, in which all may find welcome and peace.

It is important for everyone who participates in this rite to be free of expectations, to be relaxed and ordinary and open to the Spirit. To encourage this attentive waiting, it is customary to conceal the nature of what will happen, to give an innocuous title for the day that does not contain the words "contemplative Eucharist." As in the spiritual life of which it is an example, there is, once again, no "success" or "failure" in this rite. It is what it is. Each congregation and each context is different.

People and Timing

The Animator

The animator's role is delicate and costly. It involves being as empty, silent, and as unobtrusive as possible while at the same time making sure the venue is ready, the instruction given, and a minimal structure established in which people can be open, vulnerable, and deeply silent.

The animator is always a layperson.[2] This person should be a stranger to the participants, and should disappear after the rite is over so that if the rite is done on Saturday, for example (this seems to be the best day in a parish situation), the animator is not anywhere in evidence on the next day, Sunday. While she may make a thanksgiving at the end of the rite along with everyone else, she should leave the premises immediately and unobtrusively afterwards in order to eliminate the possibility that people will try to speak to her. *The rules in this paragraph are essential to the rite and cannot not be altered without changing its nature.*

The animator should confer with the vicar or organizer ahead of time to find out the layout of the venue, to ensure that there will be enough hosts on hand, and that the logistics of the rite are understood. Beyond these practical considerations, the animator should not discuss the rite so as not to impose his or her own (always provisional) understanding of it. The animator is the most vulnerable person in the rite and will be profoundly changed each time she participates in it. Ideally a person should not function as animator more than once or twice a year.

The animator has several burdens to bear. A person who lives from a radical interior silence may find any sort of public role very difficult, yet sharing this silence is the most precious gift she (or he) has to give. During the rite, the animator must have continual reference to her core silence, not only to help the participants relax and be comfortable with silence but also so that she will not be swamped or deflected by the swirl of incoming signals from the group.

The animator should have a melodious, unaffected, clear speaking voice, and the instructions and second meditation must be presented in an inviting way, but without inserting the animator's own experience or interpretation into the text by inflection or any other means. She should not hesitate to use a microphone if necessary so that she does not have to raise her voice. It goes without saying that any sort of theatricality would be totally out of place.

The animator must have the ability by use of the voice alone, and the silence that supports it, to enable the group to go ever deeper into silence. This means that the animator must be able to set aside whatever

2. Because of interpersonal dynamics it is usually preferable that the animator to be a laywoman, even (or especially) in an all-male context. The same is true for the Speaker of the Epiclesis.

other concerns might preoccupy her so that they are not communicated through her voice.[3]

The animator must consciously and repeatedly renew her trust in the Holy Spirit working through the rite and the process. This non-interfering self-restraint can be very difficult when, for example, a participant seems to be trying to take a prominent role (as with the gargoyle clerics described below), or when something else seems to go awry. It is essential to sustain the atmosphere of the liturgy, which should be able to absorb disturbances in such a way that they disappear into the flow. The animator's ability to maintain a depth of focus through all distractions will enable the congregation to do the same.[4]

The Shills

The title may be amusing, but the role is important. The animator gives the instructions only once, at the beginning of the rite. The shills' task is to help the congregation relax by discreetly providing momentum if there should be a collective memory lapse. They can be trained the day before or even a few minutes before the rite; there are only four actions to remember: to notice when the animator is ready to begin; to go to and from the silent meditations; to initiate the procession; to initiate going up to the altar to break their hosts. The criteria for choosing shills are: common sense, unobtrusiveness, comfort with silence and the ability to wait, a sensitivity and attention that is tuned into the feel of the group from moment to moment. Nine times out of ten the shills are not needed. The congregation should not know who they are nor is it necessary for them to know that they are present.

The Speaker of the Epiclesis

The Speaker of the Epiclesis says the spontaneous epiclesis (invocation of the Holy Spirit) over the bread and wine towards the end of the rite when all have individually broken their host into the container serving as a paten and have gathered around the altar. As these are the only words

---

3. See the quotation from John the Solitary in the appendix. This quotation could be copied out and posted near the refreshments.

4. In fact, I have never seen or heard of any disturbances during this rite or ones similar to it. The silence becomes too enveloping, and the absence of imposed interpretations seems to eliminate the need to disrupt.

spoken within the rite that are not spoken by the animator, it is extremely important that this person (either man or woman, but preferably a lay-woman) be sensitive enough to the group to be able to express the quality of the silence on that particular occasion in that particular congregation. In the epiclesis the speaker quietly gestures towards this quality of silence and invokes the Holy Spirit in one brief spontaneous sentence, but without imposing his or her own agenda. This way of speaking the epiclesis is much closer to the Eucharistic rite of the early churches than any rite we have today.

The speaker also assists the animator, fulfilling her requests in regard to effecting the material aspects of the rite. The speaker is also usually the person who dresses the altar between the end of the third meditation and the appearance of the group in the nave. Aside from the low-key speaking of the epiclesis, the speaker should be invisible and participate as one of the group. Strict attention to the self-effacing character of this servant role is particularly important if the speaker is ordained, for whom it will usually be more difficult than for a layperson.

It is perhaps significant that on the first occasion of the rite all the clergy present without exception had chosen to wear ordinary clothes and to be unremarkable in their behavior. In fact, they were so unobtrusive that discreet inquiries had to be made to find out if there was an ordained person present to pray the epiclesis (on this first occasion I didn't have the courage to ask a layperson). This is how the church ought to operate all the time.

It is perfectly acceptable—in fact, preferable—in this rite for a non-ordained person to say the epiclesis; it is *Christ*, after all, who makes Eucharist, and the Christ-movement of self-emptying is not confined to ordained Christians, or, for that matter, Christians in general. But this first occasion took place in an Episcopal church, and it was not the moment to make political statements or create controversy.

If the speaker is to be a layperson, she or he can be selected by the organizer of the event in advance (or by the congregation: such a group will have decided by consensus that they want to have the rite and will have requested it as a group), or else the choice can be left to the animator on the day. The animator should be discerning enough to be able to pick someone appropriate. The criteria for selection of the speaker should not be what we commonly, if erroneously, think of as "leadership qualities," but should rather center around stillness and unobtrusiveness and the ability to help others focus beyond themselves. If these criteria are followed, the choice for speaker will naturally fall to someone who is closer to the margins than to the center of the group. The rite is a lived kenosis and throws any attempt at domination into sharp relief.

On one or two occasions there have been clergy who have asked to have the rite in their churches but on finding out what it involves—or doesn't involve—are profoundly threatened. They are reluctant to let go their safe and rigid forms even for a few hours. This, too, is part of life, and rather than trying to change the cleric, the animator should remain neutral and let the chips fall, relying on the truth of the rite and the Holy Spirit working through it to enlighten the cleric. This involves a willingness on the animator's part to risk in faith and continually to renew the commitment to suspend all judgment and evaluation.

If it becomes evident that the situation is going to become too problematic for the cleric(s), the animator should withdraw the rite in advance or improvise a substitute on the spot. Because the silence in the rite becomes poised and penetrating, the slightest tension will communicate itself to the participants. The rite should not be risked in a non-receptive situation, and there are some clergy who simply refuse to listen to or grant credence to anyone else, least of all a layperson; they are reluctant to let go one iota of control. The animator should accept all of these conditions with equanimity, even if in the end she must withdraw. As Ghandi used to say, nonviolence works only in a situation where those in power have a conscience.

On one occasion at a small parish, a very defensive vicar arrived in clericals even though he had been asked ahead of time not to wear them. However, when he saw what was unfolding at the beginning of the first meditation, he vanished discreetly and reappeared even more discreetly in a polo shirt. He went on to participate with deep attention.

In another parish, the situation was more extreme: the congregation had been infantilized. They exhibited the body language of grammar school children. During the most important part of the rite, the husband-and-wife clerics who ran the parish decided to ensconce themselves on either side of the sanctuary like two guardian gargoyles in an evident attempt to intimidate, to assert the illusion of their continuing control in a situation that had already gone far beyond their control and had revealed the inappropriateness of such tactics. It was a strategy that was to backfire in a spectacular way shortly afterwards.[5]

5. Perhaps the most startling shift was from a cathedral dean who greeted me the day before the rite with, "I just want you to know that I am opposed to everything

Anyone who participates in this rite will be sifted. It should not be lightly undertaken.

Timing

While the rite is particularly appropriate for a Saturday at the beginning of Advent or Lent, or in a time of reconciliation, it can be undertaken at any season when there is no competition for the participants' energy and attention (it would not be appropriate to use during Christmastide or Holy Week, for example). However, one parish has used it for a New Year's Eve Vigil.

This rite is not designed to be a regular event. Once in a lifetime for a participant may be enough. There is no hard and fast rule about this, but memory and expectation may compromise a person's openness the second time around.

In a world of high mobility a parish might make the rite available at intervals of three to five years. The number of participants should be limited to forty-five at most. Even if only a few members of a parish participate in the rite, the quality of their interior stillness can deepen the life of an entire congregation. To paraphrase Simeon the New Theologian, one person's silence can transfigure a thousand lives.

The Venue and Its Preparation

The Venue

The preferred setting for the rite is a church with a parish hall, but almost any church or chapel can and has been used with some improvising. The essential is that there be enough space for people to do silent meditation with some sense of privacy and solitude, and also that people are not crowded when they are together. The venue also needs to have a sanctuary and an altar.

The venue should be reserved for the entire day. It is impossible to predict the amount of time that will pass until the last person has left,

---

you stand for." At the end of the rite the next day he asked me to concelebrate on the following day, Sunday, and since this was clearly the work of the Holy Spirit—and also a cathedral with a very large congregation—I agreed. I was able to disappear within and immediately after the Sunday liturgy without encountering individuals from the day before.

and it is vital that no one feel rushed during any part of this liturgy. There should be a sense of spacious leisure.

The normal gathering time is 9:30 AM with the rite starting at 10 AM. Refreshments (water, tea, munchies, etc.) should be readily available in a quiet corner where participants can discreetly help themselves until after the third meditation.

Supplies

"Priests' hosts," the sort that are wafer thin and approximately three inches in diameter, are available from convents or from commercial church supply firms. While these hosts often come with a cross or other figure stamped on them, it is important for this rite that they be blank.

There should be a supply of scrap paper and pencils in an unobtrusive place, e.g., near the coffee pot, for those who might want them.

Set-up

IN THE PARISH HALL

The gathering place should be within sight of the refreshment table, but not too close to it. Chairs should be set in a quarter-circle in several rows facing the narrow end. Each chair should have at least three feet of space all around it. There should be a lectern facing the chairs.

Logistics such as toilet locations, etc., should be dealt with informally in advance. Everything should be clearly signposted. There should be a notice on the food table that refreshment will be available throughout the morning/afternoon.

IN THE SANCTUARY

The rite assumes but does not require a free-standing altar. The sanctuary should be as open to the nave as possible. If there are portable altar rails, they should be removed, along with kneelers. Even if the rails cannot be removed, the sanctuary at least should be cleared of enough furniture so that everyone can stand around the altar. In small churches there may be a little crowding, but this does not matter. There should not be any flowers or extraneous items in the church or sanctuary. It should be as simple as possible. If there are elderly or disabled people present, chairs should be left in the sanctuary, each with a discreet sign indicating its use. The church should either have natural light or else be half-lit with artificial light. Bright florescent lights should not be used.

THE ALTAR

The altar should be bare throughout the time of the first three meditations when some of the participants may want to meditate in the church. In the short interval between the end of the third meditation and the informal procession of the congregation into the church, the altar should be set as simply as possible with a corporal (a piece of plain, clean, white linen about a foot square), a prepared chalice (wine with a few drops of water already added), and an empty paten, plate, or bowl large enough to receive all the hosts that will be broken into it. The chalice and the bowl should be as beautiful and simple as possible, e.g., a Revere bowl and a plain chalice. Glass is fine if it is not fancy. Two very simple candles should be on the altar, or free-standing as appropriate to the architecture of the sanctuary.

The Rite Begins

The Introduction

At around 10 AM when the moment feels right, the animator goes quietly to the lectern and simply stands there, waiting until people notice and sit down. No announcement is made. The people will gather quickly as by this time they are alert for the beginning of the morning's activity. It is essential that there be no request for silence or gathering. The shills can be useful here, but they should not call attention to themselves in any way or attempt to herd the others. The animator should make sure that all her movements are made slowly and gently, but without affectation.

The Gathering

When everyone is seated and quiet, the animator says gently:

Peace be with you.

*There may or may not be a response. This is unimportant. The anima-
tor continues by giving the following information slowly, quietly, and
clearly, in her own words, if possible. It is important not to give any
more or any less information than is supplied here. The instructions
may seem like a lot, but in fact take only about five minutes to present.*

Today presents us with a space of opportunity, a time of unhurried silence to dwell at the heart of the Eucharist. Each person brings something
unique to this shared silence of solitudes, and each person will receive
something unique from it. While there will be aids to meditation available throughout the day, here are a few of the questions and thoughts that
might be useful for consideration:

a. What do we mean when we say, "here we offer and present our selves,
   our souls, and bodies as a living sacrifice"?

b. What does it mean when we say with the celebrant, as we are meant to,
   "this is my body given for you"?

c. The climax of the Eucharist is the fraction, the breaking of the Bread:
   there is no salvation without sacrifice. Every true sacred sign effaces
   itself *[at this point the animator takes a host, holds it up, breaks it, and
   holds the two halves apart, keeping silence for a moment]*; that is, every
   true sacred sign gestures towards a vanishing point. For example, the
   empty space between these two halves of bread echoes the mercy seat,
   the "great speaking absence" between the cherubim.[6] It echoes the
   cave of Elijah where he heard the still small voice; it echoes the womb
   of Mary and the empty tomb and all the other empty spaces of opportunity where, released from the shackles of our perception, Love has
   infinite play with the resonances of the Word.

Whatever you find yourself doing today, take all the time you need
within the framework that is available. We will keep silence throughout
the day, and we will go home in silence. Out of respect for others' silence
and solitude, please observe what used to be known as "custody of the
eyes." When you get home, try to continue to live from the deep silence
of the heart you may find here, even if you are not able to keep silence
externally. Most important of all, please do not talk about what happens
here today, either among yourselves or with others, as talking about it

6. Rowan Williams, *Open to Judgement*, 101.

will tend to dissipate the transfiguring power of whatever you have been given.

Here is the outline of the day. These instructions will be given only once, but they are very simple and nothing can go wrong. Everything that happens is Eucharist.

At the conclusion of this introduction you will be given a host. This is the focus of your meditation for the day.

There will be three meditations. The first meditation is silent and lasts for twenty-five minutes. You may go anywhere you like to make this meditation, including the church and the garden, but please return to your seat here at the end of this time.

When everyone has returned, we will have the second meditation together. This meditation contains passages that serve as the Epistle and Gospel for today.

The third meditation is also silent, and again, you may go anywhere you like. At the end of twenty-five minutes, please return to your seat here.

After everyone has returned there will be a silence of about five minutes. Then at the signal—which you will recognize when it is given—we will process informally into the church. When we get there, please find a seat in a pew as you would normally on a Sunday morning.

Once everyone has arrived and settled into the pews and the silence has deepened, each one of us, when you are ready, will, informally and individually, and in no particular order, go one by one up to the altar and break the host each one of us has been given into the paten that is waiting there and then return to a place in the pew. *Please take as much time as you need for this action.*

Once everyone has had the opportunity to break their host at the altar, I will go forward to break my host. At this point, please leave your pew and come forward to stand around the altar.

After we have settled around the altar, a brief invocation of the Holy Spirit will be said over the elements and we will receive Communion. After everyone has received we will return informally to our places in the pews to make thanksgiving. Please take as much time for your thanksgiving as you wish.

It is important to emerge from the silence slowly and gently. When you are ready to leave, please depart the building and grounds in silence. If possible, try to live the rest of this day in silence, or at least from the core of this silence.

Once again, nothing can go wrong in this liturgy; everything that happens is part of our life, all of which is acceptable to our loving God.

Are there any questions?

There are usually one or two questions.

We will now distribute the hosts.

The hosts are passed out by the animator and an assistant, if necessary, who should not have any other role and who should not be ordained. There is a pause while everyone settles.

The animator returns to the lectern and introduces the first meditation. This introduction should be as brief as possible and should include the following information, but nothing more:

The Anglican rite for Eucharist begins with an adaptation of a medieval prayer that was originally composed for the enclosure of an anchorite, a man or woman who vowed to live out their lives of prayer enclosed in a small dwelling, usually attached to a church. In this first meditation, let us "cleanse the thoughts of our hearts" as the prayer bids us, so that we may come to a greater purity of heart and receptive listening to the inspiration of the Holy Spirit.

Once again, you may go anywhere you like for this meditation, including the church (and the garden/classrooms, etc.); please return in twenty-five minutes.

The group disperses for twenty-five minutes. The animator removes the lectern and taking a host for herself goes off to find a quiet spot and meditate with it for twenty-five minutes, just like everyone else.

At the end of that time, the animator returns slowly and quietly to the gathering place, but this time to a chair set apart at the back of the other chairs so that everyone is facing away from her. The shills should disperse themselves with everyone else and keep an eye on the time so that at the end of the meditation they can individually return slowly and quietly to the gathering place, thus encouraging everyone else to do so without in any way interfering with another's solitude. When everyone is settled the animator begins slowly and reflectively to read the following meditation:

Meditation: Forgetfulness and Creation[7]

This morning I would like to try not simply to communicate ideas to you, but rather share an experience, better, a way of being that is central and important. There will be words and images, but they are here to evoke another level of reality, which you are invited to enter. Let us therefore begin with a time of silence, because it will be silence that will be our place of communion.

[pause]

Put yourselves in a relaxed position, remaining alert. . . . Close your eyes. . . . Enter within your self. . . . Let your awareness inhabit your body. . . . Welcome the movement of your breathing. . . . Slow it down a bit. . . . Be fully and peaceably there, from the center of your being to its edge. . . . You are.

[pause]

As we continue, listen at the level of your inmost being with the ear of your silence. Let what the words evoke live in your heart.

[brief pause]

"I want to know Christ and the power of his resurrection and the sharing of his suffering by becoming like him in his death, if somehow I may attain the resurrection from the dead. Not that I have already obtained this or have already reached the goal; but I press on to make it my own, because Christ Jesus has made me his own. Beloved, I do not consider that I have made it my own; but this one thing I do: forgetting what lies behind and straining forward to what lies ahead, I press on towards the goal for the prize of the heavenly call of God in Christ Jesus."[8]

[pause]

7. Adapted from an unpublished Carthusian novice conference, my translation and adaptation.

8. Phil 3:10–14, translated from the French.

"Forgetting what lies behind and straining forward to what lies ahead, I press on towards the goal." Baptism cannot be a conclusion in an absolute sense. It is a conclusion in regard to the past; it is a point of departure in regard to the future. And Paul insists that we should strain forward to what lies ahead. The way travelled is to be forgotten: no vain remorse, no "if only," no complacency on account of hoarded spiritual riches.

[pause]

Before God we are always indifferent servants, pardoned sinners, poor ones. Let us not close our hands on nothing, but keep them open towards the Lord in order to receive the munificence of his love. We are his children in the measure that we are born of God; and it is naked that we are born.

[pause]

The power to forget is very important. It allows us to get rid of resentments and marks of honor, defilements, and exterior burdens from our past, so that we keep only what is inscribed on the substance of our being, by which we are that which we are in the present moment. Thus, casting everything aside, we can run ahead, buoyant and responsive, everything straining for the goal, which lies ahead, in a perpetual going beyond everything, never pausing in this life. "Draw me after you, let us make haste," we cry to Christ.

[pause]

Christ is always ahead. Union with God presents itself as perpetual newness, a continual beginning to begin again. We climb the ladder that links earth and heaven, the one that Jacob saw; God calls us to come up to him. The ladder is Christ, and every rung reached opens always towards something beyond. We find ourselves always beginning.

[pause]

This continual going beyond self isn't a particular stage in the spiritual life, it is the very condition of our being. The spirit, an immaterial and intelligible reality, is, in itself, unlimited. In this, God and the soul are of one nature.

[pause]

The created being can always become greater. If God is infinite in action, the soul is infinite in becoming. Its divinity consists in being transfigured into God. If it is infinite in becoming, its creation necessarily takes the form of growth, without which it would be merely finite, which characterizes the material world. In this perspective, this continual progress is constitutive of the soul itself, it keeps it always turned towards something beyond itself.

[pause]

There is something of prime importance here for our way of living day by day.

[brief pause]

Let us try another little experience. Close your eyes, breathe two or three times, deeply and slowly. . . . Become aware of your body . . . then enter into your self to the source of your being. . . . Then, sitting there peacefully, visualise yourself on the screen of your imagination. . . . See your body irradiated with light. . . . It is thus that you are wrapped in the love of God, love that gives you being in your material existence— the breath we receive expresses this well—and gives you your spiritual existence. . . . Existence as a created spirit capable of unlimited growth in knowledge and love. . . . Existence as adopted children of God, who plunges us into his own intimate life. . . . This life is communicated to us in each instant by a relationship of grace and liberty that permits us to grow endlessly in goodness and love even to the fullness of Christ, which is without end.

[pause]

Let us be aware of this light of love that surrounds us. . . . Love touches us through each object that we see, great or small: the mountain and the tree, the sun and the candle flame. . . . It sings in the song of birds, beckons in the murmur of the brook. . . . It takes a human face with Christ, but also in each human being who rubs shoulders with us. . . . It breaks into our life through all the events which form it. . . . It is constant in our heart, a presence of the Lord whose name accents our breathing. . . . We breathe the Love who creates us, here and now.

[pause]

Consciously and with confident surrender, I open myself to this life and this light which, on God's side, are eternal; the creative action of God, in God, is God himself. . . . Only its effects are in time. . . . Each present moment links me with eternity, bears me as a child to the Father in the love of the Spirit. . . . This moment is rich with the entire past, and bears in itself the future in the measure that I commit myself to it in faith. Forgetting the past, I press on wholeheartedly towards the goal, letting myself be borne by the flow of the present.

[pause]

It is precisely the reality of my actual participation in the life of God that, overwhelming me, enflames my desire and turns it towards its well-spring. . . . I turn by forgetting, by the poverty of my empty hands. . . . I soar up on my desire. . . . Each instant is an absolute beginning. . . . I receive myself anew, and I give myself in all simplicity. . . . The joy of my gratitude and my praise for the love and mercy of God that enfold me are the song of my creation.

[pause]

But that which is obtained cannot become a limit to my desire. . . . This is not God. . . . The most dazzling light, the most intense feeling of love, the greatest revelation of his beauty—this is still not the One who is infinite, incomprehensible, always beyond. . . . To be with God, I must thus go always further to encounter his newness without end.

[pause]

To reach the Creator I must myself become a creator—at least as regards the disposition of the spirit. . . . I must smash all the molds in which I continually shape myself, because they are always limited; I must reject all security, familiar words, riches, offer myself utterly poor, virgin, to the breath of the Spirit. . . . Thus is our creativity made possible, the only creativity that counts, which forms Christ in us, which gives birth; the creativity which forms us, our selves, not just any created work, but our selves, in a poem of love to God, a poem that is absolutely unique.

[pause]

Sometimes it is by solemn words of love that the Spirit gives me being, sometimes by joyous ones. There are very ordinary words: bread . . . water . . . ; there are words of humiliation, . . . of suffering, . . . even of sin. We must allow our selves to be formed by these words so that the glory of God may be sung.

[pause]

If I am the poet of the poem that is my life, I am also a priest. The Word that is given me as a Christian has the power to change everything into the Body of Christ. . . . This is my body . . . blood, poured out for you. . . . As God creates, in each instant, through his Word, he thus recreates us, reassumes us in all our humanity, with all the creation, in an eternal offering of the love of Christ to the Father, into whose heart the Eucharist plunges us.

[pause]

Let us together live a day of creation. . . . Let us enter into our selves until we come to the level from which springs the source of our being. . . . Each morning is an absolute beginning. . . . God creates the heavens and the earth in this instant. . . . I open my eyes on the morning of creation, I receive the gift of being, wholly new, from the hand of God. . . . The first movement is a surge of wonder and gratitude. . . . The sun rises. . . . We hasten to meet this Love that comes to us in the tasks and happenings of our day, however little they are. . . . Let us be attentive to the secret presence of Love that enfolds us, to its tenderness, sometimes very personal. . . . This inventive attention, this confidence and receptivity are, perhaps, a very simple form of continual prayer.

[pause]

Let us receive the words of our poem in joy and surrender to the Spirit who inspires them, whether or not they are pleasing to our ear. . . . What do we know? . . . When the words surpass our comprehension, when the melody is dissonant, unexpected, or full of half tones, we escape our limits, we go beyond. . . . This melody, these words that are so simple, so concrete, are secretly infused with the Word, bear the form of Christ, say, "Father."

[pause]

"In the beginning was the Word, and the Word was with God, and the Word was God. . . . All things came into being through him, and without him not one thing came into being. What has come into being, in him, was life and the life was the light of all people."[9]

[pause]

Each morning let us plunge our being, our day, into the torrent of Love that floods, that is, the life of the blessed Trinity. . . . This is the creation; this is the Eucharist. . . . Let us welcome, consecrate, offer our selves, our verse for today, in the eternal Eucharist, the thanksgiving to Love. . . . What is given no longer belongs to us; our offering is the passage (the Passover) of our life in God. . . . It goes through the dispossession of forgetting in the single remembrance of God, in beholding. . . . We turn ourselves, we advance in faith and confidence towards the One who comes and who will come. . . . In each instant, in each thing, person, circumstance, God communicates himself, Christ becomes incarnate, the Spirit unites in the invisible bonds of love.

[pause]

"And God saw all that was made, and indeed, it was very good, and there was evening and there was morning . . . ." In the evening, I give back my being to God; I surrender my life and entrust myself in the repose of the seventh day. . . . Each night I die in faith, having only my poverty, and

9. From the Prologue to the Gospel of John.

my trust and peace in a hope that wishes neither to count nor to know anything.

Thus we proceed, flowers of a day, "from beginnings, in beginnings, through beginnings that never end."

At the end of the spoken meditation there is a pause.

Then the animator gives the following information:

The third meditation is about offering. Towards the end of this meditation, if you wish—but it is not necessary—you might want to write down a single word on a small piece of paper and take it home and do something ritual with it: burn it in a candle; bury it in the garden; grind it up and bake it into cookies; tie it to a rock and throw it into the river or the sea.

Once again, you may go anywhere you like for this meditation. Please return in twenty-five minutes.

Everyone disperses including the animator. At the end of twenty-five minutes, everyone returns. The animator once again goes to the back of the chairs. When everyone is settled and the silence has deepened the animator gives the signal.

The signal that is normally used is a gloss on Julian of Norwich, chapter 5 of the Long Text, but it can be changed according to the circumstances:

"And Julian looked at the small round thing in her hand and realized that it was everything that God had made: that God loves it, God sustains it, and God keeps it."[10]

Everyone rises slowly and processes informally into the church, where each finds a place in a pew, facing the altar. The shills assist this movement simply by initiating and being part of the group movement. When everyone is settled there is usually a space of silence before the first person is moved to go forward and break his or her host into the receptacle on the altar. The animator and the speaker stay at the back of the church to ensure that every person has had the opportunity to go forward.

---

10. Julian of Norwich, *The Revelation of Love*, 7, my translation.

This is usually the moment in the rite when it is most difficult to wait, when it is most difficult for the clergy to trust the laity and the rite (not to mention the animator!) and at which the shills need to be most sensitive so as not to jump the gun. It is important to let the silence deepen and not to rig either the process or the outcome.

This is also the point in the rite at which there will be the most variation. Some people will take off their shoes. Others will get to the altar steps and seem terrified to go any further. They must be given all the time they need.

It is also at this point that there may be variation of other kinds: elderly people may need to be helped up the steps, if there are steps, and should be able to remain in the sanctuary without obstructing the sightline—and the solitude—of the action at the altar or of the people who are sitting in the pews, who have either broken their host or are waiting to do so. It is at this point also that some people simply "forget" to go back to the pew, though never in my experience has the central action or the flow of the liturgy ever been interfered with. In any event, these variations are part of the process and there should be no attempt at regimentation.

If there are a lot of participants, the process of going forward one by one will take a long time, though it will not seem long because of the action at the altar.[11] When the last person in the pews has gone forward and come back, the speaker goes forward and remains discreetly behind or to the side of the altar. Lastly, the animator goes forward, and as she breaks her host, the rest of the congregation comes forward to stand around the altar. The speaker stands closest to the elements behind the altar, facing the nave, with one of the shills standing unobtrusively nearby.

When everyone has settled and the silence has deepened, the speaker prays over the gifts with a one-sentence, spontaneous epiclesis. It should be no more than one short sentence, and it should gesture towards the action of the Holy Spirit who unceasingly consecrates the lives who have broken the hosts and placed them on the altar.

After the speaker has prayed the one-sentence invocation over the gifts, there is another pause to simply be in the silence. Then with unhurried movement the speaker communicates the nearby shill, who slowly distributes the Bread, making sure that each person gets two halves. The speaker reaches for the chalice and faces the nearest person who has already

---

11. Forty-five people take a little more than an hour and a half to perform this part of the ritual on average.

received the Bread and waits reverently while they drink from it and pass it on to the next person. *All communicate in silence.*

When the Bread returns to the altar the shill communicates the speaker. They should leave any fragments. Anything left over can be dealt with by those who clear the altar, which should not take place until the last person has left the nave after the thanksgiving.

The speaker is also the last to receive the chalice. When he or she sets the cup back on the altar after receiving, everyone slowly and informally moves back to their places in the pews, the speaker and the animator going again to the west door of the church. At this point they may melt into the group, sitting in the back pews to make their own thanksgiving, but they should slip away before anyone is tempted to come and speak to them.

People will sometimes stay a very long time at the end of the rite. The doors to the nave should be shut to protect their silence. They must not be rushed or disturbed. Only when the last person has left the church may the altar be cleared and the furniture set back in its normal configuration, if it has had to be moved.

There is usually a lot of energy around at the end of the rite, and people sometimes forget to be silent. If participants attempt to speak on their way out they should be gently discouraged with a silent, gentle nod and renewed attention toward the altar.

There should be no scheduled follow-up to this rite, no discussion, no evaluation, no attempts to elicit responses from the participants. "Loose ends" are to be welcomed as sources of rumination and deepening, and no effort should be made to tie them up.

Variations

No written rite can allow for every circumstance. As long as the basic structure, principles, and presentation of the rite are unchanged, it can and should be adjusted according to need.

For example, in a service for the sick, the signal might be Jesus' saying that he comes not for the well but for the sick. In such a service, the movement by which the participants break their hosts into the paten would have to be improvised.

In an ecumenical situation where intercommunion is forbidden, the signal could reflect the pain of division. After each person has broken their host into the paten or bowl provided (the chalice will have been prepared ahead of time as usual), the rite can be ended, the group remaining in silence until one by one they drift away, the rite having no communion and no conclusion.

In such a situation the signal could reflect the severity of the disunity. On one occasion, the rite was to be used for a meeting of a local ARCIC group. Two days before the meeting, the very conservative Roman Catholic bishop of the area not only refused permission for intercommunion on this one occasion, he did so in a public and extremely hurtful way.

On this occasion the signal was: "And though I give my body to be burned and have not love, I am nothing." At the end of the aborted rite when everyone had left, the animator took the broken hosts away and burned them privately, as there was no place at the venue to burn them publicly. This conclusion had been agreed upon ahead of time by the organizers, and had been described during the introduction to the rite.

In the end, any group that uses this rite must decide how far it is able to go forward in trust and faith. The more participants are able to risk in silence, the greater will be the possibility for transfiguration.[12]

Adaptation for Regular Use

There are a growing number of parishes offering an alternative Sunday Eucharist that is simpler and quieter than the main service of the day. Many of these Eucharists are somewhat effective, but most of them lack contemplative leisure and are still too wordy.

While there are a number of alternative liturgical possibilities available today, an increased amount of silence does not seem to be one of them because the clergy are afraid that the laity are uncomfortable with silence. Yet it is silence that attracts worshippers to these alternative services, and they should be satisfied.

There is no reason that an alternative Sunday Eucharist should not incorporate the main elements of the rite outlined above, including the

---

12. The bridging of the abyss between clergy and the non-ordained could be greatly facilitated by using this rite at clergy conference, with an unknown layperson as a Speaker of the Epiclesis, in addition to the animator, who is always a layperson.

central act of one-by-one breaking a host into a paten on the altar, as the numbers of people attending these alternative services are usually few.

Such a service should omit all explanations, attempts to make people "comfortable" (which usually end up making people squirm with embarrassment and destroy the prayerful atmosphere), since the people coming to this service already know more or less what to expect. The service might have the bare-bones elements listed below, with everything said or read slowly and thoughtfully, but without seeming studied or artificial.

For such a rite, a brief printed explanation of the rite could be place on the table that holds the hosts at the chapel entrance. The Confession, the psalm, the Peace, the announcements, the homily, the Collection, and all but bare bones elements of the canon are omitted. One or both of the lessons could also be omitted with only the Gospel for the day being read.

The rite might then proceed as follows:

Each person coming into the sanctuary or chapel picks up a host and takes it with them to their seat (along with an explanatory leaflet, if desired). Then follows:

a) a prayer for purity of heart, either the traditional Anglican one or one that is improvised, although it would be hard to improve on the simplicity of ". . . cleanse the thoughts of our hearts by the inspiration of thy Holy Spirit . . ." This collect would be followed by a silence of two or three minutes.

b) the Collect for the day, followed by an even longer silence.

c) the reading(s), followed by a significant silence (at least five minutes); each reading (if there is more than one) begins abruptly with no introduction or interpretation and with no closing salutation.

d) the homily should be omitted. This is a service in which people want to listen to what the silence has to tell them individually about the reading(s)

e) the intercessions, which should not be a long and formal laundry list, but simply a quiet voicing of particular concern, which should be begun and summed up in great humility by the celebrant/animator in a prayer that leads into an offertory sentence followed by a long silence.

f) one by one each person breaks a host into the paten and steps back from the altar (though not going back to their seat) until all are gathered at the altar.

g) after a silence the speaker spontaneously prays a very simple version of the words of Institution and/or a one-sentence epiclesis appropriate to the assembled group and reflecting the common concern

h) all receive Communion

i) the remains are left on the altar while all return to their seats to sit in silent thanksgiving. The congregation leaves individually in silence.

Basic Principles

The liturgical form outlined above is only a suggestion. Each group should adapt the silent Eucharist to its own needs. The basic principles underlying both the long and the short forms are:

a) the primacy of silence before, during, and after each liturgical action/reading/gesture; silence as the matrix from which the Word (and ourselves) come and to which the Word (and ourselves) return (cf. Isaiah's "it will not return empty"); very slow reading and movement, without being artificial

b) the equality of all self-offering before God

c) letting the Word/liturgy/silence speak for itself without interpretation

d) a physical gesture of self-offering at the altar—the breaking of the host that will then be given as Communion—made by each participant.

Those who think that the laity are "not ready" for silence or that they need to have the liturgy explained to them *ad nauseam* should witness the Compline service that has been held at St Mark's Cathedral in Seattle for more than fifty years. It began when some graduate students in music asked if they could sing Compline in the nave, just for their own edification. Gradually attendance at this service swelled until today the cathedral is filled to capacity each Sunday evening. The doors open at 9 PM and the people, whose average age is twenty-three, flow into the building until the pews are filled and people are sitting everywhere in the pews and on the floor, including the sanctuary.

The cathedral is dimly lit; the youthful congregation is respectful and silent—and have turned off their mobile phones without anyone telling them to. There are no clergy, no announcements, no welcomings, no interpretations, no organ prelude. Promptly at 9:30—the service is broadcast to a large audience on radio and the Internet—the choir enters

in silence, sings a modified version of Compline, interspersed with mo-
tets, and then leaves in silence. The congregation departs (more or less)
in silence.

Although the Eucharistic liturgy presented in this book evolved inde-
pendently from this Compline service, it is put together along similar
lines. It seems astonishing that clergy who know of this Compline service
have not noted its "success," that they have not thought to take the pages
of silence and the effacement of their role from its book; that they have
not incorporated more silence and less of themselves, that is, less interpretation (interpretation which is often intrusive and unhelpful) into the
regular liturgies they conduct.

Modern people live at a tremendously fast pace in a culture of noise
and artificiality. We are continually assaulted by those who tell us how
and what we ought to think. Liturgy, more now than other time in history, has the urgent task and the precious opportunity of helping us to
stop, to be silent, to enter the heart of God, which lies at the center of our
own nature.

Peace be with you.

Appendix
John the Solitary (fourth century):

"How long shall I be in the world of the voice and not in the world of the
word? For everything that is seen is voice and is spoken with the voice,
but in the invisible world there is no voice, for not even voice can utter
its mystery. How long shall I be voice and not silence, when shall I depart
from the voice, no longer remaining in things which the voice proclaims?
When shall I become word in an awareness of hidden things, when shall
I be raised up to silence, to something which neither voice nor word can
bring."[13]

---

13. Quoted in Brock, "John the Solitary, *On Prayer*," 87.

FIVE[1]

Behold

Behold! I have given you every herb . . . and every tree . . . and every beast . . . and every fowl . . . and every thing that creepeth . . . . (Gen 1:29–30)

Behold! I have seen the suffering of my people. (Exod 3:7)

Behold! I am laying in Zion a foundation stone. (Isa 28:16)

Behold! I am sending my messenger. (Mal 3:1)

Behold! the bridegroom comes. (Matt 25:6)

Behold! You shall conceive. (Luke 1:31)

Behold! I bring you good tidings. (Luke 2:10)

Behold! the Lamb of God. (John 1:29)

Behold! the hour comes. (John 16:32)

Behold! I show you a mystery. (1 Cor 15:51)

Behold! he is coming with the clouds and everyone shall see him. (Rev 1:7)

Behold! the Lion of Judah. (Rev 5:5)

Behold! the tabernacle of God is within you. (Rev 21:3)

---

1. Parts of this chapter was originally included in a paper that was requested by Vincent Gillespie, "Behold Not the Cloud of Experience" (2013). It was a prequel to the two papers on which we collaborated after many years intensive study of Julian of Norwich's text: "The Apophatic Image: The Poetics of Effacement in Julian of Norwich" (1992) and "'With mekeness aske perseverantly': On Reading Julian of Norwich" (2004). (Details on all publications can be found in the bibliography.) I am also indebted to John Barton, Oriel and Laing Professor of Biblical Interpretation at Oxford, for conversations over nearly three decades, though any errors are entirely mine. Some paragraphs from "Behold Not the Cloud" appeared in Volume 1, but are worth repeating for the sake of context. However, I have omitted the textual/translation analyses already presented.

THE WORD BEHOLD IS arguably the most important word in the Bible and by extension in spiritual life, which it epitomizes, and its significance is transmitted through the early history of Christianity into the Middle Ages. *Behold* is not an archaic word; it is still used intuitively and correctly, if infrequently, in the media and in ordinary conversation. I have even seen it used in advertising, e.g., "Behold! Our New Sandwich Menu!" Despite this currency and the word's centrality to the biblical text, it has been dropped from most modern translations of the Bible, changing and draining the essential meaning and theology of many passages, and negatively affecting the modern interpretation of medieval texts.

The English word *behold* accurately conveys the many psychological and theological nuances of both the Hebrew (*hinneh*) and Greek (*idou, theōreō*) from which it is translated. *Hinneh and idou* stand in the same slightly odd relationship to their ancient tongues that *behold* does to English.[2] In Old English *bihalden* signifies "give regard to, hold in view," also "to keep hold of, to belong to," from "by" ("thoroughly") + *halden, healdan*. It is related to the German *halten* "to hold," originally "to keep, tend, watch over." The Old English also has connotations of friendly, gracious, loyal, kind. As *behold* is a liminal word, the paradox of intention applies: one *holds* or *grasps* by *ungrasping*: in beholding, the analytic, conceptualizing faculty is relinquished.[3]

"Behold" is a word that alerts us to pause, however briefly, to be vigilant, because something new, something startling, is about to be revealed. Beholding is a process of continual death (the mind being temporarily brought to silence) and resurrection (the arrival of a new perspective). If we live in beholding we continually live in a new creation.

With the word *behold*, it is as if we are given not only direct perception but also the ability to see beyond the appearances to the divine radiance itself that we, in beholding, share with God. Our beholding of God imparts to us that radiance. St Benedict's *Rule* has a thread of this glory running through it, a thread that is usually ignored in the darker translations of the contemporary age.

But there is another aspect to this glory-bestowing Word which we behold: *logos* can also be translated as, "the inward meaning which is expressed in speech, the sense of something, its coherence; orderedness that is both implicate and emergent"[4] It is not unreasonable to think that

2. John Barton, private conversation.

3. Shaw, *The Paradox of Intention, passim.*

4. Personal communication from Mark Williams.

the author of John's Gospel is using *logos* in both senses: it is through the divine exchange of beholding that meaning is given to us, and it is in listening for the Word in deep silence that this meaning appears in our speech and enables our two kinds of knowing to work harmoniously together. Equally, the meaning of our speech—always fragmentary, a gesture—is enhanced and amplified when it is returned to deep silence to be refined and trans-figured in the direct perception of the glory of God that consents to dwell there.

God truly makes a home with us, to share the divine nature as Word, as meaning and as glory, and all of this comes through the word *behold*. The resonances of beholding are not only contagious, they are also amplified by our being in beholding in the world. Beholding is a manifestation of the deep mind; it is enduring and helps us live our contemplation in an ephemeral world.

We are at a dangerous crossroads, for once the epistemological balance between silence and dialectic has been compromised, it is difficult, very difficult, to restore; for noise by definition obliterates silence. These days we are pressured on all sides by the noise of twisted minds spinning in closed loops. The babble used to sell their crazy agendas is persuasive because most listeners have no experience of silence, and therefore have no intellectual or emotional autonomy through which to critique the insanities and inanities on offer. But this is exactly what politicians and corporations want, because if we stopped to balance our lives with a little transfigurative silence and beholding, we might become aware that we are rapidly becoming their slaves.

Behold is the first and primary covenant word from which all else derives. As we have seen, it is the first word that God speaks to Adam and Eve after he finishes creating and blessing them (Gen 1:29), the word he uses throughout the Bible to recall his people to himself: the books of the prophets are littered with the word. *Behold* in the Judeo-Christian tradition entails all of religion, spirituality, morality, and ethics. The one who beholds faces outward, self-forgetful, engaged, and contiguous with the community of the beheld; beholding is holistic receptivity and engagement.

The summary of Israel's Law, the *Shema'* (meaning "Hear!"), is a statement of beholding (Deut 6:4–5). The legal code, while a gift, is secondary to beholding. As in any religion, a legal code is easily abused as a concession to practitioners who refuse to behold, who use it to increase self-regard, which objectifies, dehumanizes, and distorts religion—of any sort—which then becomes hierarchical and compartmentalized. The prophets excoriate this vitiated religion, condemning cults and codes that enable people to take refuge in a comfortable religious materialism; that allow them to watch themselves with approval, reassured that they are righteous.[5]

Jesus, in the tradition of the prophets before him, taught people to free themselves from these tendencies by returning to the beholding that precedes the giving of the law. He makes this purpose explicit in Luke 17:21: "The kingdom of God is not coming with signs to be observed, neither will they say, 'Behold! here it is!' or 'Behold! there it is'; for, behold! the kingdom of God is within you" (cf. Matt 24:23). This teaching is echoed in Matthew 24:26–27 and Mark 13:21. The third phrase of Luke 17:21, "'behold, the kingdom of heaven is within you,'" is highlighted in the Greek. This highlighting is picked up by Jerome and occurs in some modern translations (e.g., as in the plodding NRSV "for in fact") even where the word *behold* has been replaced by an analytical word such as *look*. Post-Enlightenment translators, having lost the word *behold*, seem to find this passage incomprehensible. Modern scholars seem largely to have ignored its centrality in the contemplative tradition.

Luke 17:21 is in the background of Irenaeus' (second century) famous saying, "The glory of God is the human person fully alive, and the glory of the human person is the beholding of God,"[6] and the "late have I loved you" passage in Augustine's *Confessions* X.27.38. *Behold* is fundamental to Gregory of Nyssa's theology.[7] Cassian quotes Luke 17:21 in Conference 13 immediately following the remark equating distraction with fornication.[8] Isaac of Nineveh (seventh century), drawing on much

---

5. See, for example, Isa 1:10–17; Jer 6:20; Amos 5:21–23; Mic 6:6.

6. Irenaeus, *Adversus Haereses* 4:38.

7. Daniélou, *From Glory to Glory*, 100–101; P.G. XLIV 1269C–1272A.

8. *Fornication* in the Bible refers far more often to worshipping false gods than it does to sexual activity. Modern studies often seem to overlook this primary sense of the word, which is passed down through Cassian to the monastic tradition of the later Middle Ages. "But we ought to be aware on what we should have the purpose of our mind fixed, and to what goal we should ever recall the gaze of our soul: and when the mind can secure this it may rejoice; and grieve and sigh when it is withdrawn from this, and as often as it discovers itself to have fallen away from gazing on Him, it should admit that it has lapsed from the highest good, considering that even a momentary departure from gazing on Christ is fornication. And when our gaze has wandered ever so little from Him, let us turn the eyes of the soul back to Him, and recall our mental gaze as in a perfectly straight direction. For everything depends on the inward frame of mind, and when the devil has been expelled from this, and sins no longer reign

earlier writers, insists that the kingdom of heaven has always meant contemplation.[9] This sense also occurs in Richard of St Victor's *The Mystical Ark* III. 5, 10; it is alluded to in Walter Hilton's *Scale* II.33; and its sense pervades *The Cloud of Unknowing* and Julian's Long Text. For these authors, beholding is the *process of en-Christing*. Jesus was a person; Christ is a process. "The philosopher *par excellence* and philosophy itself is Christ: *ipsa philosophia Christus*."[10]

Beholding is threatening to institutions. In John 14:17–19, Jesus tells his disciples that while they can behold (*idou*), the system (*kosmos*) cannot behold (*idou*), and because the system cannot behold (*idou*) it cannot receive the Spirit of Truth or know it. *Kosmos* is usually translated *the world*, but the Gospel of John is about Jesus as the new temple and by extension the human heart as the holy of holies. Jesus is alluding with particular irony to the temple system in the context of worldly systems in general, systems that are by definition confined to the linear and the hierarchical, which are alien to beholding. It is not hard to see why the medieval church came to regard the Bible as a very dangerous book indeed, or why the institution increasingly insisted on external observance and pious devotion at the expense of contemplation.[11]

The word *behold* occurs more than 1,300 times in the King James Bible. Although the seventeenth-century committee was making a word-for-word translation, they did not use *behold* in many verses where it would have been appropriate: "behold me" (e.g., Isa 6:8) is translated "here am I," a move that effects a significant shift in theological and personal meaning. This paraphrasing has continued in subsequent translations: *behold* has disappeared from most English Bibles since the Revised Standard Version (1946–57), and with it have vanished the contemplative

---

in it, it follows that the kingdom of God is founded in us, as the Evangelist says 'The kingdom of God cometh not with observation, nor shall men say Lo [*ecce*] here, or lo [*ecce*] there: for verily [*ecce enim*] I say unto you that the kingdom of God is within you.'" Cassian, *Conferences*, 1:13; translation www.osb.org/lectio/cassian/conf/book1/conf1.html#1.13.

9. Alfeyev, *The Spiritual World*, 267.

10. LeClercq, *The Love of Learning*, 101.

11. Contemplation—strictly speaking, attentive receptivity—excludes interpretation. One has to be careful with the words *contemplation* and *meditation*: Luther changed the word *contemplation* to refer to an abstract intellectual process (see Vol. 1). Also, Buddhists use *contemplation* in a similar way, as an equivalent to *rumination*, while they use *meditation* more in the sense of attentive receptivity that excludes interpretation.

threads that are woven into the original languages.[12] Just as *behold* is the first word of covenant God speaks to his newly created people after he has blessed them (Gen 1:29), so *behold* is the first word of covenant of the new creation, the last word that the risen Christ speaks to his disciples: "Behold! I am with you always, to the end of the age" (Matt 28:20b). It is in the beholding itself that he is with the disciples.[13] From a psycho-theological standpoint, beholding is a living, ongoing recapitulation of the self-emptying en-Christing process of Philippians 2:5–11. Without the *behold* at the end of Matthew's Gospel, the understanding of Christ's nature and engagement with the world changes completely.

Instead of *behold*, the New Revised Standard Version uses *remember*, which makes Christ history. In the ancient sense, remember carried the meaning of participation in what was being remembered. But in the modern sense, to remember means that Christ is no longer "living and active" (Heb 4:12). Instead he is now literally re-membered, that is, reconstructed as an artifact instead of being lived through beholding. *Remember* in its modern sense has nothing of the covenant of engagement, self-emptying, or mutual indwelling entailed in *behold*. *Remember* rather entails a Promethean attitude: the one who is remembering is cut off, is over and against. *Remember* seeks to circumscribe and control. This substitution debases the text and raises the question, *how* is the risen Christ with his people until the end of time? The NRSV translators have taken Matthew's restatement of the first and still living covenant of Genesis 1:29 as it transfigures into the covenant of the new creation, and transformed it into an isolated memory that reduces those Jesus leaves behind to abandoned and alienated orphans, a denial of the promise in John 14:18.

Behold is *the* marker word in the Bible. It interrupts the narrative to keep the reader's mental processes in the boundless present. It prevents interpretation from becoming too abstract, linear, and schematized; it opens on the deep mind, which is not directly accessible.[14] In both ancient and modern Hebrew, *behold* says far more than "Pay attention!" It signals the conflation of the two different points of view of the self-

12. The NRSV uses *behold* only twenty-seven times in the Old Testament and Apocrypha, and not at all in the New Testament.

13. This is Bernard's understanding in Sermon 31 on the Canticle III.7. Migne, *PL* 183.940–45; *Bernard of Clairvaux: Sermon on the Song of Songs*, 124–33.

14. The deep mind can be accessed only indirectly; it can be influenced primarily by intention, paradox, and resonance, by meditation and contemplation, and by some of the literary tropes described in this volume.

conscious mind and the deep mind (right side of the diagram in Vol. 1, 34–35), the irruption of the deep mind's insight into liminality. It alerts the reader to radical new meaning, a merging of time and timelessness, of *chronos* and *kairos*; it frees the reader from the bondage of time-bound self-consciousness to receive a glimpse of the ineffable, however fleeting. It signals a shift of perspective, a turning inside-out and upside down; it emphasizes what today might be called the counter-intuitive. This sudden shift of perspective creates an aporia that holds the mind in stillness and self-forgetfulness, engaged and responsive without analyzing or interpreting.

As these different epistemologies, these paradoxical perspectives are opened to one another, there is, as it were, an explosion of silence and light, a silence in which the person is engaged, held in thrall, in stupefaction. These words do not indicate catatonia or trance or unconsciousness, but wide-awake direct perception: beholding is normative, in the same way that the Orthodox are wont to say that the disciples' beholding on the Mount of Transfiguration is normative.[15]

"The contemplative does not see God," writes Simon Tugwell, "he enters into God's seeing."[16] Contemplation shifts the center of the person from self-consciousness to the deep mind; it changes physical appearance, relationships with others (*Cloud*, chs. 54; 55.25–32; 61; 63.11–27)— even the person's smell becomes different, as does his or her engagement with the natural world.[17]

Beholding is not the same as mindfulness. Mindfulness is a practice; it can elide into beholding, and it can enhance the capacity for beholding. But beholding is beyond human control. It is gratuitous, just as the insight and other effects that may emerge are gratuitous. It is possible only to be open to beholding, to have beholding irrupt into and displace the interpretive diversions of what is called *experience*.[18] *Conversion* means turning away from the distractions of experience and their noise; it means

15. See particularly the icon written by Theophane the Greek: in the vignette on the left, the disciples follow Jesus up the mountain; in the vignette on the right, descending from the mountain, Jesus and the disciples are in a group, as per John 15:15. "I no longer call you servants, because the servant does not know what his master is doing; but I call you friends, because I have made known to you everything I have heard from my Father." (Icon available at image databases online.)

16. Walsh, *The Cloud of Unknowing*, xxii. See Irenaeus' statement above about the reciprocity of beholding.

17. Isaac of Nineveh, tr. Sebastian Brock, in *The Fountain and the Furnace*, 185–86.

18. *The Book of Privy Counselling* (hereafter *PC*), 81.40–82.1; 82.10–14.

continually choosing to "seke [him] to beholding" (Julian, ch. 10).[19] It is from beholding that the self-conscious experience that constitutes daily living optimally derives its energy and to which it continually returns.[20]

Beholding is *embodied*; it opens on the deep mind where incarnation, transfiguration, and resurrection are rapt into one. The body signals beholding by the *orans* gesture.[21] To behold entails a reciprocal holding in being. God the creator of all, God who is beyond being, consents to have his creatures hold him in being in time and space, even as God is holding them in time and eternity (*Cloud*, ch. 4). God who *unfolds* the creation *enfolds* it to his heart (*beclosyth* in Julian, ch. 5 and following). This notion of exchange is intrinsic to beholding, even extending to and including sin, which is less possible to commit as the center of the person is moved from the feedback loop of self-consciousness to self-forgetful immersion in the free upwelling from the deep mind.[22]

———

Beholding sums up everything that has gone before in these two volumes; it is the background, context, and goal of everything I have written. Beholding is not necessarily religious; there can be "secular" beholding as well. But whether it is secular or religious, to cultivate beholding and its matrix of silence in deep mind is not an option: it is absolutely necessary to human well-being, and it becomes a way of being in the world. If we are to have any possibility of surviving as a species, much less living

19. See Gillespie, "The Colours of Contemplation," 7–28.

20. In chapter 82, Julian describes the optimal circulation between self-consciousness and the deep mind: "And I understode that while we be in this life, it is full spedefull to us that we sen both these at onys; for the heyer beholding kepith us in gostly solace and trew enioying in God; that other, that is the lower beholding, kepith us in drede and makith us ashamyd of ourselfe." Pseudo-Denys similarly insists on the necessity of the kataphatic to the apophatic (plurality and simplicity, procession and return). See Rorem, *Biblical and Liturgical Symbols*.

21. This is the prayerful posture in which one stands (usually) with elbows at one's sides and hands, palms up, stretched out to the side.

22. Sin is a function of self-consciousness. The modern "true self/false self" dichotomy (the latter needing to be destroyed or suppressed) has insinuated itself anachronistically into academic studies of medieval texts. It is a process of self-judgement that takes place entirely in the self-conscious, conceptual mind. It is not only *not* a medieval notion, it is not even a Christian notion (Matt 7:1), as everything created is good, and "synne is behovabil." It is no accident that Julian's statement comes in chapter 27, immediately after she enters the glorified wound in the side of Christ into apophatic beholding, which she celebrates in the doxology of chapter 26. It is in the beholding itself that "al manner of thyng shal be wele" (Ch. 27).

optimally with the right hemisphere in healthy relationship to the left, that is, deep mind slightly predominating over self-conscious, linear mind, then we must have more silence in our lives and especially in our surrounding physical environment. We cannot be in right relationship with our selves, other people, other creatures, our environment without beholding.

To make the world more aware of beholding, to weave beholding into our ordinary lives, is a gargantuan task. It requires a shift away from the consumer culture that is eroding our humanity. The churches could help if they would, but the clergy are terrified of silence and it is futile to look for help in that quarter; the clergy presume (in the worst sense) to retain their sense of superior status, which is not only antithetical to the Christianity they purport to teach, but increasingly destructive to both the institution and the people who make it up. Institutional Christianity needs to be reformed from the ground up, from the entrenched, corrupt, and corrosive power systems to the liturgy. Christianity needs a new Bible translation that restores the poetry and contemplative strands and the word *behold*. It needs new liturgies that honor the apophatic and the role of silence as the highest form of praise of God (St. Ephrem). These items only scratch the surface; much more is needed. If these reforms are not undertaken, then people will continue to drift away from churches until there are only clergy left, talking to themselves in their empty buildings. It is not a situation that fosters optimism.

Fortunately, beholding is not dependent on the institution. Anyone can undertake the work of silence and receive the gift of beholding. It requires only an openness and receptivity, a relinquishing of the complex blandishments and noise of a consumer society for simplicity, silence, and self-forgetfulness, a turning away from narcissism to welcome the other. The work of silence is so simple, yet to go against the grain of society and the culture is very difficult. But it is worth the effort: the work of silence and the way of being in the world that is beholding provide stability and even joy in a disintegrating world. People who undertake to live like this become beacons, islands of safety where others can find a refuge. The resonances of silence permeate the world around them, whether they are aware of them or not. To paraphrase Julian of Norwich, seek [him] to the beholding, and everything shall be added unto you: peace, joy, glory.

Select Bibliography

Ackroyd, Peter. *Blake*. London: Folio Society, 2008.

Alfeyev, Hilarion. *The Spiritual World of Isaac the Syrian*. CS 175. Kalamazoo, MI: Cistercian, 2000.

Augustine, Saint. *Confessions*. Translated by Henry Chadwick. Oxford: Oxford University Press, 1992.

Barker, Margaret. *The Great High Priest: The Temple Roots of Christian Liturgy*. London: Bloomsbury T. & T. Clark, 2003.

Barnes, Julian. *Keeping an Eye Open: Essays on Art*. London: Cape, 2015.

Barthes, Roland. *The Pleasure of the Text*. Translated by Richard Miller. New York: Hill and Wang, 1975.

Barton, John. "God, the World, and Wisdom." In *Within the Love of God: Essays on the Doctrine of God in Honour of Paul S. Fiddes*, edited by Anthony Clarke and Andrew Moore, 19–28. Oxford: Oxford University Press, 2014.

Bernard of Clairvaux. *Sermon on the Song of Songs*, vol. 2. Translated by Kilian Walsh, OSB, and Irene Edmonds. Kalamazoo, MI: Cistercian, 1983.

Bertold, George C., ed. *Maximus Confessor: Selected Writings*. Introduction by Jaroslav Pelikan, preface by Irénée Dalmais, OP. New York: Paulist, 1985.

Brock, S. P. *A Garland of Hymns from the Early Church*. Mclean, VA: St Athanasius, 1989.

———. "John the Solitary, *On Prayer*." *Journal of Theological Studies* 30.1 (1979) 84–96.

———. *The Luminous Eye: The Spiritual World View of St Ephrem*. Kalamazoo, MI: Cistercian, 1992.

Buber, Martin. *I and Thou*. Translated by Walter Kaufmann. Edinburgh: T. & T. Clark, 1970.

Casey, Michael. "Bernard's Biblical Mysticism." *Studies in Spirituality* 4 (1994) 12–30.

Cassian, John. *Conferences*. Book 1, chapter 13. www.osb.org/lectio/cassian/conf/book1/conf1.html#1.13.

Chase, Steven. *Angelic Wisdom: The Cherubim and the Grace of Contemplation in Richard of St. Victor*. Notre Dame, IN: Notre Dame University Press, 1995.

Clifford, Richard J. *Psalms 1–72*. Abingdon Old Testament Commentaries. New York: Abingdon, 2002.

Combes, André. *Ioannis Carlerii de Gerson: De Mystica Theologia*. Lugano, Switzerland: Inaedibus Thesauri Mundi, 1958.

Cranz, F. Edward, et al. *Nicolas of Cusa and the Renaissance*. London: Routledge, 2000.

Daniélou, Jean. *From Glory to Glory: Texts from Gregory of Nyssa*. Yonkers, NY: St Vladimir's Seminary Press, 1997. (PG XLIV 1269C–1272A)

Fanous, Samuel, and Vincent Gillespie. *Companion to English Medieval Mysticism.* Cambridge: Cambridge University Press, 2011.

Fenton, John. *Finding the Way through Mark.* London: Mowbray, 1995.

Fretheim, Terence. *The Suffering of God.* Philadelphia: Fortress, 1984.

Furedi, Frank. *Power of Reading: From Socrates to Twitter.* London: Bloomsbury, 2015.

Gerson, Jean. "Epistle 26." In *Oeuvres complètes, Introduction, texte et notes par Mgr [Palémon] Glorieux,* vol. 2, 98. 10 vols. Paris: Desclée, 1960.

Gillespie, Vincent. "The Colours of Contemplation: Less Light on Julian of Norwich." In *The Medieval Mystical Tradition in England VIII,* edited by E. A. Jones, 7–28. Cambridge: Boydell and Brewer, 2013.

————. "Postcards from the Edge: Interpreting the Ineffable in Medieval English Mystics." In *Interpretation: Medieval and Modern,* edited by Piero Boitani and Anna Torti, 137–65. Cambridge: Brewer, 1992.

Gillespie, Vincent, and Maggie Ross. "The Apophatic Image: The Poetics of Effacement in Julian of Norwich." In *The Medieval Mystical Tradition in England V,* edited by E. A. Jones, 55–77. Cambridge: Boydell and Brewer, 1992.

————. "'With mekeness aske perseverantly': On Reading Julian of Norwich." *Mystics Quarterly,* 30 (2004) 125–40.

Gleick, James. *Chaos: Making a New Science.* New York: Vintage, 1987.

Golitzin, Alexander. *Mystagogy: A Monastic Reading of Dionysis Areopagita.* Kalamazoo, MI: Cistercian, 2014.

Harmless, William, S.J. *Mystics.* New York: Oxford University Press, 2008.

Harwood, Britton J. "Langland's 'Kynde Knowyng' and the Quest for Christ." *Modern Philology* 80.3 (1983) 242–55.

Heschel, Abraham Joshua. *The Prophets.* London: Bravo, 2001.

Hirshfield, Jane. *Nine Gates: Entering the Mind of Poetry.* New York: HarperCollins, 1998.

————. *Ten Windows: How Great Poems Transform the World.* New York: Knopf, 2015.

Hodgson, Phyllis, ed. *The Cloud of Unknowing and The Book of Privy Counselling.* Oxford: Oxford University Press, 1973.

Isaac the Syrian. *Ascetical Homilies of Isaac the Syrian.* Translated from the Greek. Boston: Holy Transfiguration Monastery, 1984.

Julian of Norwich. *The Revelation of Love.* Edited by Marion Glasscoe. Exeter, UK: University of Exeter Press, 1993.

Kaminsky, Ilya, and Katherine Towler, eds. *A God in the House: Poets Talk about Faith.* North Adams, MA: Tupelo, 2011.

Krava, Martin. *Jewish Messianism and the History of Philosophy.* Cambridge: Cambridge University Press, 2004.

LeClercq, Jean, OSB. *The Love of Learning and the Desire for God.* Translated by Catharine Misrahi. New York: Fordham University Press, 1982.

Lee, Li Young. "The Subject Is Silence." In *A God in the House: Poets Talk About Faith,* edited by Ilya Kaminsky and Katherine Towler, 120–33. North Adams, MA: Tupelo, 2011.

Lewis, C. S. *A Preface to Paradise Lost.* Oxford: Oxford University Press, 1954.

Levinas, Emmanuel. "Textes Messianiques." In *Difficile liberté,* 3rd ed., 119–20. Paris: Livre de poche, 1984. (Translated by Seán Hand as "Messianic Texts," in E. Levinas, *Difficult Freedom: Essays on Judaism.* Baltimore: John Hopkins University Press, 1990.)

Louth, Andrew. *Dionysius the Areopagite*. London: Bloomsbury Academic, 2002.

Lunn, David. *The English Benedictines: 1540-1688: From Reformation to Revolution*. London: Burns and Oates, 1980.

MacKendrick, Karmen. *Immemorial Silence*. New York: SUNY, 2001.

MacCulloch, Diarmaid. *Silence: A Christian History*. London: Allen Lane, 2013.

McCann, Daniel. *Soul Health: Therapeutic Reading in Late Medieval England*. Cardiff: University of Wales Press, forthcoming 2018.

McGilchrist, Iain. *The Master and His Emissary: The Divided Brain and the Making of the Western World*. New Haven: Yale University Press, 2012.

McGinn, Bernard. "'Evil-Sounding, Rash, and Suspect of Heresy': Tensions between Mysticism and Magisterium in the History of the Church." *The Catholic Historical Review* 90.2 (2004) 193-212.

Moltmann, Jürgen. *The Crucified God: The Cross of Christ as the Foundation and Criticism of Christian Theology*. Translated by R. A. Wilson and J. Bowden. London: SCM, 1974.

Pseudo-Dionysius: The Complete Works. Translated by Colm Luibheid and Paul Rorem. New York: Paulist, 1987.

Rahner, Hugo. *Man at Play*. Translated by B. Battershaw and E. Quinn. London: Burns and Oates, 1963.

Rorem, Paul. *Biblical and Liturgical Symbols within the Pseudo-Dionysian Synthesis*. Toronto: Pontifical Institute of Medieval Studies, 1984.

Ross, Ellen M. *The Grief of God: Images of the Suffering Jesus in Late Medieval England*. New York: Oxford University Press, 1997.

Ross, Maggie. "Apophatic Prayer as a Theological Model: Notes for a Quantum Theology." *Literature and Theology* 7.4 (1993) 325-53.

———. "Behold Not the Cloud of Experience." In *The Medieval Mystical Tradition in England VIII*, edited by E. A. Jones, 29-50. Cambridge: Boydell and Brewer, 2013.

———. *The Fountain and the Furnace: The Way of Tears and Fire*. 1987. Reprint. Eugene, OR: Wipf and Stock, 2014.

———. "Jesus in the Balance." *Word and World* 29.2 (2009) 152-61.

———. *Pillars of Flame: Power, Priesthood, and Spiritual Maturity*. San Francisco: HarperSanFrancisco, 1988.

Ryrie, Alexander. *Silent Waiting: The Biblical Roots of Contemplative Spirituality*. Norwich, UK: Canterbury, 1999.

Shaw, Marvin. *The Paradox of Intention: Reaching the Goal by Giving Up the Attempt to Reach It*. Oxford: Oxford University Press, 2008.

Short, Coyote. *Spirit of Eagle Rock: A Native American Cultural and Geologic Interpretation of Eagle Rock*. Eagle Rock/Boise, ID: Idaho Museum of Mining and Geology, n.d.

Sutcliffe, Tom. "In Defense of Shakespeare's Difficult Bits." *The Guardian*, 6 January 2016.

Tsoknyi, Rinpoche. *Carefree Dignity: Discourses on Training in the Nature of Mind*. Kathmandu, Nepal: Rangjung Yeshe, 1998.

von Rad, Gerhard. *Old Testament Theology, Vol. I*. New York: Harper and Row, 1965.

Walsh, James, ed. *The Cloud of Unknowing*. Preface by Simon Tugwell. Mahwah, NJ: Paulist, 1998.

Williams, J. P. *Denying Divinity: Apophasis in the Christian Patristic and Soto Zen Traditions*. Oxford: Oxford University Press, 2001.

Williams, Rowan. *Open to Judgement: Sermons and Addresses.* London: Darton, Longman, Todd, 1994.

Wollheim, Richard. *Painting as an Art.* Princeton, NJ: Princeton University Press, 1990.

Wright, N. T. "*'Harpagmos'* and the Meaning of Philippians 2:5–11." *Journal of Theological Studies* 37 (1986) 321–52.

Zinn, Grover, tr. *Richard of St Victor: The Twelve Patriarchs, The Mystical Ark, Book Three of the Trinity.* New York: Paulist, 1979.

Made in the USA
Middletown, DE
12 May 2018